Flim-Flam Man

A True Family History

Jennifer Vogel

SCRIBNER

NEW YORK LONDON
TORONTO SYDNEY

SCRIBNER
1230 Avenue of the Americas
New York, NY 10020

For information about special discounts for bulk purchases,
please contact Simon & Schuster Special Sales:
1-800-456-6798 or business@simonandschuster.com

Designed by Kyoko Watanabe
Text set in Minion

Manufactured in the United States of America

10   9   8   7   6   5   4   3   2   1

Library of Congress Cataloging-in-Publication Data
Vogel, Jennifer.
Flim-flam man : a true family history / Jennifer Vogel.
    p.   cm.
1. Vogel, John Bryson, 1942–1995. 2. Criminals—United States—Biography.
3. Fugitives from justice—United States—Biography. 4. Vogel, Jennifer.
5. Adult children of dysfunctional families—United States—Biography.
6. Fathers and daughters—United States—Case studies. 7. Problem families—
United States—Case studies. I. Title.
HV6248.V64V63   2004
364.1'092—dc21
[B]   2003057255

ISBN 0-7432-1707-1

For Mom

"I wish I was able to buy you a new car or a home or something, but I'm a little short right now, honey."

Dad from prison, 1987

Flim-Flam Man

The funeral was a shambles

I DROVE MY ESCORT through the gates of St. Vincent cemetery, a small, well-manicured plot of land practically invisible amid the highways and chain restaurants of Minneapolis's northern suburbs. I passed tidy beds of marigolds and petunias, a towering ivory Jesus on a cross with three fretting women at his feet. The rutted trail wound through rows of stones like jack-o'-lantern teeth and finally met the upright granite slab that reads *Vogel*. The family plot, until now inhabited solely by my grandmother Margaret, rests in back next to the drainage ditch.

That Grandma was buried alone here is a testament to my family's overall instability, a history exploded to bits. We hold grudges, disown, deny, and pretend at easy glamour. We start over and wipe slates clean. What is passed down is something nobody wants to own, so that each new generation darts ahead, dodges the shadow, breaks the link, only to be gripped for all time just as our mothers and fathers tumble backward into darkness.

Grandma had been poor, shanty Irish she called it, Catholic. She'd attended Mass on Saturday nights, a ritual of absolution before heading to the bars. She used to strut up to the church—teased red hair, brightly drawn lips—puffing a cigarette. With long fingernails, she'd flick the butt into the bushes on her way through the door. Then she'd dip her tarry fingers into the holy water.

1

Grandma sent my father to Catholic school; Dad was even an altar boy at the Basilica of St. Mary in Minneapolis. Eventually, he'd revolted. So vehemently had he resented the Church's hypocrisy that he'd wound up a devout atheist. He was fond of imitating priests: "Louder, boy!"

On this 95-degree July afternoon, with mosquitoes attacking, my father would be laid out under the cross next to his mother, drawn back into the fold.

The sky was thick and hazy white and I thought it might sink down and smother me as I walked, stabbing the grass with high heels, toward the tiny, unsatisfactory group gathered to mourn Dad. Under my new black-and-white dress, I felt the rolled band of my panty hose. It was creeping up my waist, swallowing me like an anaconda. I tugged at it, but could hardly breathe.

Off to the right, just beyond a chain-link fence, I noticed five or six people gathered for a barbecue outside an apartment complex situated too close to the graveyard. They were giving off sounds of ice jiggling and laughter as one or another hummed jokes and stories. Hamburger smell wafted in our direction. People like another species.

The mood on my side of the fence was grim. The casket, traveling some 250 miles from a funeral home in Sioux Falls, South Dakota, was late, leaving the mourners with nothing to fixate on but each other. At the core of our anxious entourage was my father's younger sister, Cheryl. Cheryl had helped support Dad in recent years and was the one who'd driven out to identify his body under fluorescent lights. She felt intense proprietorship over the funeral. She'd made the arrangements. There was no money, so there was no church, no organ music, and no program (the funeral home would forget the bookmark-size cards she'd ordered). My father's send-off consisted of a few carnations, a prayer for "the poor captive souls in Purgatory," and a huddle of folding chairs next to an Astroturf-covered hole in the ground. I studied the hole. I imagined it an ancient mouth that had been whispering obscenities to Dad his whole life, stripping away little pieces until there was nothing left but his corpse. Now it was going to devour that too.

Cheryl had been highly selective with the invitations. She'd included her two kids, Dad's hapless younger brother, Tom, my sister and me, and a small cadre of my father's more respectable friends. Despite a routine of robbery, arson, insurance fraud, and counterfeiting, Dad had managed to keep lifelong pals: people happy to forgive or ignore all manner of transgression as long as they were having a good time. Dressed in rumpled suits, my father's compatriots looked like washed-up salesmen, beaten down but still tricky. They milled about and lifted their sweating faces in praise of Dad, figuring it was the appropriate thing to do. "John was *such* a great guy," declared a half-blind chronic alcoholic. I remembered that this man had visited our lake cabin during summers. Once, around the Fourth of July, he'd started a motorboat in the shallow water and broken off all the propeller blades. "He could figure anything out," the blind man assured us, "solve any problem."

"There will never be anyone else like John," added a distinguished-looking man with salt-and-pepper hair. He'd been in prison with Dad when the two were teenagers. They'd fired guns together and even pulled a few scams. Once, they'd purchased a miniature golf course, sold it, and then packed it up in the middle of the night and sold it again. "Look at the way he managed to outrun the police," he said. "For more than five months! He was so smart, they didn't know what to do with him!"

This clutch of mourners chatted uneasily, all of us remnants of Dad's fucked-up life, trying to resolve memory into a cohesive remembrance. We were a tangle of secrets and grudges and requests to look the other way—accomplices all, witting or unwitting didn't matter. He'd drawn us in. Dad could charm like that, with his shy smile and winter blue eyes. He was terrible, really, a crooked cheat. But he was brilliant too, ingenious and sometimes genuinely good. He showed me the ocean for the first time. He once bought me baby ducks. He baked lemon meringue pies. He couldn't think before coffee in the morning.

My father didn't leave behind much in the way of possessions: some clothes, two copies of a novel he'd written, and a box of mementos—a sentimental man's collection of letters and photos and torn report cards. The bulk of what remained was not in fact physical, but psychic. Dad's death set off a wide swath of internal hurricanes, perilous swirls of anger, regret, and shame. Everybody blamed everybody else. And we all blamed ourselves. Just for a little while, Dad got to be innocent.

Mom and my younger brother, Nick, who lived on either side of a small Iowa farming town, opted not to drive out for the service. Mom had done the explaining. Dad and Nick had been estranged since Nick was a boy. He didn't wish to start up a relationship now. Mom, for her part, preferred to sort through muddled emotions in private. She'd been the ex-wife longer than she'd been the wife.

That left my sister, Liz, and me. She'd arrived at my apartment two days before the funeral, worn and tight, her blond hair tied back into a hefty ponytail. Her eyes looked flat, like stickers of eyes. I assembled a couple of turkey sandwiches, which we picked at and then ignored. We sat silent at the dining table watching the circus of squirrels jumping from tree to tree outside. Then she turned to me, brimming with tears. "I keep picturing him at the end. He must have been so lonely."

The death of a father, of a crucially important person, drags you to a secret place, imparts secret knowledge. It trivializes everyday matters and separates you from everybody else. You feel abandoned by the living and kinship with the dead. You feel superior because you've tapped into this enormous sadness that's always there. People look dumb. They talk dumb. They act dumb. Liz and I drove downtown in the Escort, a college graduation present a few years earlier from Mom and her husband, Charles. Enshrouded with conspiracy, we walked into a department store and purchased two pairs of huge, black sunglasses. We wore them in disguise.

When Liz and I are in the same room, we laugh often and Phyllis Diller–loud. She is three years my junior, smart, stylish, and daring. The same sparks set us off. Once, in Hawaii, we laughed at the antic gestures of a lifeguard as we unknowingly swam inside the feeding radius of a tiger shark. Thankfully, we could now traverse this sad terrain together.

We cried and reminisced in wavering voices about the old days. We talked about summers at the cabin on Round Lake in Brainerd, Minnesota, and birthdays and Christmases and, sensibly, how there was no way we could have saved Dad, even though we both secretly wished we could have and, at least in my case, believed I should have. Time expanded and contracted, and late on the afternoon before the funeral we sat at a bar near my apartment and downed straight shots of Jim Beam. Getting drunk was like salve on a blister. It pushed the truth far away so we could see it. The two of us passed out and woke hours later with empty, complaining stomachs. At three o'clock in the morning, we back-combed our hair into bouffants, painted our faces with makeup, put on church-quality dresses, and drove to Embers. We ate basted eggs as people just off the graveyard shift stared.

I watched Cheryl walk away from the grave, light a cigarette, and lean against her car, her head bowed. Liz and I followed. "Are you okay?" I asked, my hair still absurdly ratted. She looked up with red-rimmed eyes, her face swollen, as though she'd been brutalized. "You know," she said, "John used to sit by the phone on his birthday, waiting for you kids to call. He wouldn't leave the house. I'd try to get him to go out for dinner or even to the store and he'd say 'No, they might call.'" I gaped at Cheryl. My sister started to sob. Heavy helpings of guilt are a staple among Dad's family. His mother served it to her kids, Dad served it to us, and now Cheryl was wielding the big spoon. The Vogels believe people can't be counted on to feel sadness or remorse of their own accord.

Uncle Tom must have heard what Cheryl said because he appeared before Liz and me. He stood compact, like an Irish jockey, his reddish brown hair blown straight back as usual. His blue eyes swam in his head. "I couldn't get along with John toward the end either," Tom said. "He was like a different person. Nobody could be around him." Tom isn't a very reliable man, but those words of exoneration were some of the kindest anyone has ever uttered to me.

I was mad at Cheryl for a long time after the funeral, especially when I discovered the following summer that she hadn't put a stone over Dad's grave, even though Liz and I had given her money for one. When I saw the site, I burst into tears. My father was under the grass without a raised hand to indicate where exactly. I called the cemetery and ordered a stone. I worried over what to put on it. A good friend suggested, "In forgiveness there is peace," but Liz didn't like that. She didn't want people walking by and saying, "Geez, I wonder what happened there?" I opted for a simple inscription, *John Bryson Vogel, 1942–1995.* According to the scheme of the family plot, I should have put "son" at the top of the stone, but, in my mind, the Vogels had let Dad down. I wanted to divorce him from the family.

The hearse pulled into the cemetery and approached deliberately. My eyes fixed on its glossy black coating. I wondered what it would be like to drive such a conspicuous car across the state, a dead person in back, passing families on their way to picnics and fathers mowing lawns. Did the men escorting Dad's body stop for coffee? Did they hum along to the radio? Did they make bets on the number of people who'd show up for the service?

We helped the drivers unload the plain gray box onto a gurney. The casket was a budget model, a Vantage made of twenty-gauge steel, nonsealing. Still, it was better than the plywood-and-cloth numbers reserved for the truly destitute or despised. "Would anyone like to see John, to say any last words before we commence?" the taller of the two drivers asked, his voice properly solemn. I stepped forward, clutching a photo and a note my sister and I had written, both sealed in an envelope tied with ribbon. The photo was a color shot from the Brainerd cabin. Dad is kneeling before a giant bush of orange day lilies, a brilliant blue sky behind, the three of us kids on his lap. My brother, Nick, has his fingers up behind my head, giving me a set of rabbit ears.

Dad,
    We forgive you for all the bad things you did. You showed us that the world is full of possibility and we will always love you for that.

Jennifer and Liz

The tall driver unfastened the casket's lid. "We were told not to make him up," he said, preparing me. "We did all we could, given . . . the circumstances."

I hadn't spoken to Dad in over four years. He'd become an abstraction, a cartoon. I'd joked that if he ever purported to be dead, I'd march up to the altar at his funeral and stick my head into the coffin to make sure his body was really there, to make sure the whole flowered affair wasn't part of an intricate scam to bilk an insurance company or dodge a beating.

That comment now seemed so brutal. Contempt had dissipated like fog. Images of Dad flashed and disappeared, a guerrilla slide show of parkas, kittens, blue water, cigarettes, birthday cakes. The succession of images struck progressively deeper and finally froze on Dad, tan and shirtless in cutoff Wrangler shorts, sitting in a lawn chair working a crossword puzzle. He'd spend hours with a pen, filling the squares sequentially because jumping ahead was cheating. A cigarette smoldered in his hand and a drink sweated on the table beside him. I was there too, long brown hair, skinny legs, blue bikini, pleading with him from the end of the dock to come swimming. "You go first, honey," he said with a teasing smile. "I'm right behind you."

Ah, the grip. The same as had seized my father and grandmother and her parents and their parents before that. Sweet memories whispered into the ear, emotions stirred; all to lower your defense, so the package can be slipped into your open, beseeching palms. The gift, beautifully wrapped, nicely weighted, bottomless. The box containing questions and mysteries and memories of the future, to be forever picked through and sorted. I was my father's daughter. Denying it was pointless.

I stared down into Dad's face surrounded by off-white satin. The top of his head was wrapped with a white bandage to hide the bullet holes, one at each temple, giving him the aspect of a Civil War casualty. His eyes were soft purple and his mouth was relaxed into what almost looked like a smile. In fact, he appeared more peaceful than I'd ever seen him, as though death had been a genuine relief. There would be no more worrying or hiding for Dad, no more sitting in the living room with the shades drawn, an inch-long cigarette ash hanging from his fingers. My father was finally released. And the world was free of him. I imagined that he would have worn this serene face in life had he been a more honest person, the sort who bounced grandchildren on his knee and hosted Sunday dinners.

I looked for a long time, doing my best to remember. The high forehead. The long lashes and slightly arched eyebrows. The pronounced, flat cheekbones. Then I lifted my cement arm with my crane body and slipped the note into the coffin, laying it on Dad's chest, just below his left shoulder.

I counted to three. I gave the okay to close the cover.

Early February 1995

2

FIVE MONTHS EARLIER, two U.S. marshals had found their way to my door. Their arrival wasn't a surprise. They'd first gone to my previous address and talked with my former roommate Kelly, a rock climber who lived a very above-board existence. Kelly phoned immediately to alert me that she'd given the marshals my new address. She was breathless and excited and dying to know what the agents were after. Her questions were annoying. I informed her that this wasn't a TV drama, for fuck's sake. It was 6:30 P.M. when the marshals pressed the button on my building's intercom system.

"Ms. Vogel?"

"Yes."

"I'm Agent Kawaters from the U.S. Marshals Service. My partner and I would like to have a word with you if that's all right."

"Ah . . . Okay."

"Would you mind if we came up?"

"Actually, well, I'd prefer it if you didn't. I'll come down. I'll be right there." I didn't want the marshals inside my apartment; I didn't want them sitting on my sofa, where I might be compelled to offer them hot beverages. Nor did I want them examining my belongings and making assumptions.

I'd been on edge for a week, ever since reading the front page of the daily Metro section, which featured an abysmal picture of Dad. The photograph had stopped me like a sinkhole. He looked decades older than the last time I'd seen him and terribly, incredibly sad. His defeated eyes gazed past sagging eyelids straight into the camera, as if saying to me personally, "See. See what's happened. I've had nobody." The weight of his past and the certainty of his future were right there in the photo. The accompanying article was brief. My father had been arrested a month earlier at his print shop just west of Minneapolis for counterfeiting. He'd printed nearly $20 million worth of $100 bills. He'd been passing the bills for months: $45,000, the police figured, in eighteen states. Experts described the fakes as "excellent bogus money." The article said Dad had been indicted, but had failed to show for his hearing. He'd left town, apparently, and remained at large. Authorities were embarking upon a nation-wide search. Any leads were appreciated.

My allegiance rested firmly with my father and I had no intention of helping the police put him in prison. He was my blood, after all, one of the few people I really, deeply knew. We'd been close once. When I was sixteen, he'd rescued me, provided a warm place to live complete with pepper steak dinners and a king-size waterbed. We'd even road-tripped to Seattle together and moved into a town house on the edge of Lake Washington. The marshals knew this. That's why they'd come to my door.

I wouldn't have helped them catch even a stranger. If families harbor secrets and build walls against the world, families like mine harbor grand secrets and build walls against the police. I'd been skeptical of badges ever since I could remember. Lawmen always seemed the sort who wanted to wreak havoc and do as they pleased but lacked the courage. Or, worse, they *were* breaking laws and hiding behind their guns and nightsticks to do it.

Those who are relieved by the sight of a squad car rounding a corner or the glint of a badge in a crowd seem to have an understanding with the police I can't fathom, based on property and reputation and respectable jobs and pants with neat hems. I, on the other hand, have always been the type the police are dying to arrest. Criminal by nature, like it's only a matter of time. One big slipup and I'm in jail for the rest of my life. It's what's passed down. A mark.

I had successfully parlayed my skepticism into a career. For four years I'd been a reporter for a politically aggressive weekly newspaper called *City Pages*. I wrote about the slow erosion of civil liberties and made it my personal mission to uncover corruption and other types of disreputable behavior among officers of the Minneapolis Police Department. In late 1994, I'd published one of my best pieces, a feature-length story entitled "Hit Parade" that revealed which officers had cost the city the most in civil suits. I'd unloaded all the details: the cops who were caught driving around with two drunk Indians in their trunk; the lieutenant who threw a flash-bang grenade into an apartment during a drug bust and burned an elderly couple to death; the naked sergeant who pulled a gun in a massage parlor after a hand job and later claimed to have been executing a raid. Just before the report had gone to press, I'd come home to find my living room window shot out.

The bullet remained lodged in the window's wooden frame as I pulled on my jacket, gloves, and boots and walked down two flights of stairs to the front door. I saw the marshals before they saw me. They were standing in suits under the circle of light emanating from the ceiling fixture, talking with tight mouths, their hands stuffed into their pockets. When I drew within range, they both looked up and smiled wide, friendly smiles. Agent Kawaters was of medium build with reddish hair, a meticulously trimmed beard, and pale eyes. He looked deeply clean, almost translucent. His partner was stockier, with dark hair and dark eyes. He looked like Fred Flintstone.

I pulled open the door, and each shook my hand and introduced himself.

"How about if we talk in the car?" suggested Kawaters. "It's right outside."

I looked toward the street and spotted a boxy, charcoal sedan with plain silver hubcaps. It was one of those cars that screams POLICE! "Sure," I said, "that would be fine."

They opened the car door and I slid into the backseat. The moment the door clicked shut, I panicked. What was I doing in the back of a cop car? What would I say? It occurred to me at once that I didn't have to say anything. I wasn't under arrest. These two wanted information—they'd come courting. Maybe I could even glean a few details about the search for Dad. The agents hopped into either side of the front seat. Kawaters started the engine and spun the heater knob to high. They turned sideways toward the center of the car to face me. It was dark, except for the lighted dash. A very intimate setting.

"I imagine you know why we're here." Kawaters did most of the talking.

"Yes, I know. I really . . . I can't believe it. How much was it again?"

"Almost twenty million."

"Jesus!" I let out a sharp, barking laugh.

I felt a pang of pride at the magnitude of Dad's crime; his was the fourth largest counterfeiting bust in U.S. history. Making fake money isn't easy. Nor is it common. The craft takes patience, precision, and talent. To be good—really good, not just photocopier adequate—you have to make negatives, meticulously carve masking materials, and burn metal plates. You have to line up the plates perfectly so they print on register. You have to be exact in mixing ink shades. An eye for paper color and weight is crucial. And you've got to print and print until you get it right. It turned out that Dad had taken the extra step of embedding tiny security threads in his bills. It was just like him to aim for perfection.

My father should've worked harder at being a legitimate artist. He was genuinely good. He used to sculpt clay busts that looked like something Michelangelo would have created, except that the faces were often twisted, as though looking through fire. And he sketched all the time—complicated pen-and-ink drawings of beautiful, dour-looking faces on the backs of napkins and scrap paper. He sent some comics to *Playboy* once, but they weren't accepted for publication. I assume that's because, while well rendered, they were in poor taste, even for *Playboy*. One cartoon was of a bear commenting on the funny smell inside a cave, which was really a huge vagina. Dad didn't have much faith in his artistic skills. Down deep, he didn't believe he had much of value to say to the world. Besides, how were those talents going to get him where he wanted to be financially? It's an ironic question now.

"I'd like to have one of Dad's bills as a souvenir."

The agents were amused by the request. "Ah, I don't think that's possible. All the bills will have to be destroyed."

"You couldn't just slip me one? I promise I won't cash it."

"No, I'm sorry."

Silence.

"How did you catch him, anyway? The news reports have been short on details."

"The Secret Service arrested him. Our job is to find him."

"Oh, so you're like bounty hunters. Except I guess you don't get a reward, just a paycheck."

"Yes, I guess you could say that." Again, they seemed amused. "The way John's arrest came about was, well, he made what you might call a fatal mistake. From Brownsville, Texas, he mailed a package to his shop up here. The package turned out to contain plate negatives, which are used to make counterfeit money, a roll of hundred-dollar bills, and cocaine. He'd hidden these items in two aerosol cans with false bottoms."

A postal clerk had apparently become suspicious because of something Dad did or said at the counter that day. She'd called in a couple of Customs agents, always on hand in Brownsville, a border town, and they'd loosed a dog named Narco on the box. The dog sniffed out the cocaine, which gave the police probable cause. After discovering the hidden contents of the aerosol cans, Customs alerted the Secret Service, who repacked the box and sent an agent dressed like a delivery guy to Dad's shop. Cheryl, who ran a mailing service next door, signed for the package. A few minutes later the police executed the raid. They discovered presses, paper, ink, even fresh bills lying out to dry. My father was there too. He admitted everything on the spot and was hauled off to jail. The police posed for photos surrounded by packages of Dad's bills and cracked obvious jokes, calling him a "self-made millionaire." Then, in a move that was authentically funny, they released Dad on an unsecured bond—that is, without bail—pending trial, allowing him to skip town.

The police might have been less inclined to release him had they discovered the storage locker a few days sooner. They rolled open its door to find 196,114 counterfeit hundred-dollar bills and scads of household items: twenty-one telephones, forty-six boxes of golf balls, eleven irons, six fishing poles, sixteen can openers, nine mixers, three juicers, six Scrabble games, thirty-nine stuffed animals, four hair dryers, twenty-eight watches, and more. Much more. The police thought Dad was collecting goods to open a store, but that wasn't it. He'd seen a television news report that accused Wal-Mart of moving into small towns and lowering their prices until they'd run competing mom-and-pop stores out of business. The strategy so infuriated Dad that he developed a vendetta against the company. While his counterfeiting operation was in high gear, he couldn't pass up a Wal-Mart. He used the chain to trade his homemade $100s for authentic $50s, $20s, and $10s.

My father was no Robin Hood, but he had a soft spot for mom-and-pops. It was an unusually consistent point of honor. I remember once, when I was nine or ten, he and I took a walk down the wooded path that ran past our cabin in Brainerd. We wound up at a little store run by an old couple, part of a resort on the lake. Dad bought me a candy bar. About halfway back, I tore open the package to discover that worms had chewed into the chocolate. I wanted to return the candy bar immediately, demand a new one. Dad walked me back to the store, but rather than pointing out the worms to the woman behind the counter, he purchased a replacement and made a crack about kids and gobbling. After we left, he told me how important it is to support the little guys. If I didn't, he said, the world would be overrun by impersonal chain stores, big conglomerates that don't give a rat's ass about anybody. By giving those old folks our twenty-five cents, we were doing our part to preserve a free society.

"It wasn't very smart of the police to let Dad go."

"They didn't think he was a flight risk. He's pretty well rooted here. He's got family. His sister. You. Say, you haven't heard from John, have you?"

"No. I doubt he'd call me. We haven't spoken in a long time. He thinks I'm . . . let me see if I can remember his words, 'cold and heartless.'"

"We think he might come to see you."

"Why would you think that?"

"We have a letter he wrote to you."

"Really? What does it say?"

"Something about being sorry for the way things turned out. I don't recall exactly. The Secret Service has the letter. It's part of their investigation."

It made me angry that the police had read the letter. It made me even angrier that they wouldn't tell me what it said. The letter was private, not "part of their investigation." I imagined the sad, sentimental wording. It probably attempted an explanation. It likely touched on the good old days. Dad used to confide in me. We'd linger over a plate of moo goo gai pan in a Chinese restaurant and he'd explain his views and innumerable insecurities. "I never think anything I do is good enough," he'd say. "You're my favorite," he'd say. "We're alike," he'd say. Then he'd snap open his fortune cookie and declare either "Woman who fly upside down have crack up" or "Yankee pig, you will die." He thought that was hilarious.

"I'd like to see the letter."

"I'm sure that would be possible once the investigation is over."

"Would you please make sure of it?"

"We'll do what we can."

I'd been in the car with the agents for about a half hour when my landlord, Frank, pulled up in his big blue Mercury. Somewhere in his sixties, Frank was short and paunchy, with greasy hair and horn-rimmed glasses. For decades he and his wife had taken care of the brownstone where I lived. Frank had a shop in the basement where he was building a Valentine's Day bed frame for his wife, complete with carved wooden hearts painted pink. He lavishly decorated our building each time a holiday came around. He also collected weather vanes, which were mounted in a tangle on the roof. Frank shuffled past the car and peered into the backseat window. I waved in a manner I hoped looked casual. He waved back, but I know he thought I was in some kind of trouble.

"It would be best for John if he turned himself in."

Silence.

"For safety's sake. So something really bad doesn't happen. We're not the Minneapolis police. We'll take care of him." The agents had obviously read the writing I'd done for *City Pages*. I wondered what else they knew about me.

"I really doubt I'll hear from him."

"Well, if you do, please let us know. Is there anyone else we should talk with?"

"Not that I can think of."

"Would you put us in touch with your mother?"

"I can ask her to call you."

"That would be great." Kawaters passed me a business card.

"Mind if we stop back?"

"No, I don't mind."

I exited the car and strode through the dark to the front of my building. I turned and saw that the agents were still sitting in the sedan at the curb. The engine was running and exhaust sputtered softly out the back. The two weren't looking at me. They were hunched over, scribbling notes.

We moved to a remote farmhouse

3

I HAVE NO RECOLLECTION of Dad from before I was three. The years prior are shadows cast by scraps of paper, secondhand stories, photographs. I have a picture of him in a pressed suit and tie, riling the fat, tiger-striped cat splayed on my lap; we're both laughing. I can't tell whether it's day or night. I can't tell whether he's getting up from the sofa or sitting down. And no matter how hard I look, I can't decipher whether our interaction is genuine or staged for the camera. There are stories to suggest that he doted on me during the earliest years of my life, that he thought me the most beautiful baby ever born, despite my Eisenhower-size forehead. I'm told he proudly wheeled me around the neighborhood in a stroller, stopping for anyone who wished to rub my chin and spit out a *coo-chi-coo*, and that he toted me to work with him at the lightbulb company where he was a door-to-door salesman. I'm told also that I adored the attention, so much that I insisted on being held very close to the chest. Any embrace deemed less than intimate drew long, piercing wails. Apparently, I wished to remain a baby forever. I refused to walk, though I could rattle off fairly complex sentences. I continued to suck from a bottle even after Nick, my junior by over a year, had moved on to a sippy cup.

It was at three that, in blurs and flashes, I began recording events to memory. That was the year, 1970, that Dad moved me, Mom, Nick, and Liz, just an infant, from Minneapolis to an abandoned sheep farm near Annandale, Minnesota. The farmhouse had long been vacant and the kids from town considered it either too spooky to approach or the ideal partying spot, depending on their age. Leaves had piled like snow against the wide front steps and many of the windows were broken out.

The house was three stories tall with a dormered attic at the top, but it had the feel of a much larger place. It stood imposing on a hill, surrounded by old oaks that had stopped growing just as they reached the roof's peak. Built along straight lines, the house was almost perfectly square if you took into account the double-decker wraparound porches. The porches were picketed with spindly pillars that grinned menacingly at anyone who approached the front door. In summer, the porches were encased in rusty screen, but in winter, you could walk right off the floorboards and land on your back in the yard. Inside were six bedrooms, a mammoth fireplace made of big round stones, and a grand oak staircase that started on the third level and wound down like a spine until it splayed elegantly to meet the main floor.

Mom and Dad spent months repairing the farm. Dad opened an account at the hardware store in Annandale. Trucks laden with lumber and windows and stacks of paint cans motored slowly up the long driveway. The deliverymen appeared genuinely pleased that my parents were putting such care into the old place. They stepped from their trucks and looked the house up and down, shading their eyes with their hands in salute. Sometimes they whistled and shook their heads. Dad stood on the gravel in his shorts and loafers with no socks, one hip chucked out, talking with the men. He was tall and thin and tanned brown. He waved a lit cigarette as he spoke. The men laughed on cue.

My parents stood atop tall ladders with scrapers in their hands for entire afternoons and sometimes into the dark, when it wasn't safe to stand atop tall ladders. They hammered into place bright new pieces of wood and shaped fields of carpeting with razor blade knives. They replaced the broken windows and painted the entire structure gray with white trim. Dad insisted on yellow doors for accent. The house began to look beautiful, as though it'd never been haunted at all.

My family, however, was no match for the farm. We were too small and loosely bound together to inhabit such an expansive property. We may as well have been vagabonds who'd accidentally happened upon it, dragging in our meager belongings, playing house among the ringing echoes of families much grander and heartier. We moved furniture and toys and clothing into the most desirable rooms and left the others empty. It was easy to disappear among the vacant caverns, to get yourself into trouble without anyone knowing.

Nick and I were fascinated with the attic, painted white and honeycombed with closets. We designated one particular closet the Store because it had a Dutch door that split into two parts, a top and bottom. Nick was usually the storekeeper and I the skeptical customer. One afternoon, we were dickering over the cost of grass and rocks when I caught a glimpse through the nearby window of a white glob stuck out on the roof. I walked to the window, which was smudged and dirty and had a long crack at eye height. I pointed for my brother to look. The two of us peered at the mysterious white clump growing out of the roof like a mushroom. We jimmied open the window with a butter knife and crawled out, one after the other.

There was no wind, but I stuck close to the wall of the house, never before having been so high off the ground. After a little testing, I discovered that my feet clung to the warm shingles. I moved toward the white clump. My brother was already there, down on his haunches like a farmer examining corn sprouts, staring at it. He grabbed the clump rather suddenly with both hands and began pulling.

"It's underwear!" Nick declared. He stretched them out with

some difficulty—they were dried stiff—and held them against his scrawny body approximately where a pair of underwear would go. They hung past his knees.

I moved in for closer inspection. The clump turned out to be a pair of extra-large men's Fruit of the Loom briefs. Streaked brown from rain and infested with seeds, they'd obviously been lying on the roof for some time.

"Yuck, put those down."

"I'm gonna wear 'em." Nick lowered the white-and-brown underwear as if to slip a leg into a leg hole.

"Don't you—" I snatched them from my brother and flung them over the edge.

I could see everything from the roof: the expanse of our patchy yard and the gravel driveway where my red tricycle lay on its side; the dented plastic swimming pool in which I kept the turtle Dad had picked off the asphalt; the clothesline, where towels hung like dead geese; the buildings and broken-down structures that surrounded our house—three decaying garages and an empty, rusting water tower. Beyond that, stretches of a two-lane road peeked from between dense trees. The blue water of Lake Sylvia glistened. I saw land crisscrossed with barbed-wire fence. I knew that through the pastures were trails, some obvious and some hidden, leading to milkweeds and raspberries and the foundation of a burned building. The foundation reeked of charred garbage, but if you plugged your nose and scavenged hard enough, you could find treasure. I'd once unearthed a tiny, golden ballerina.

A group of brown and white cows luxuriated under a tree in the pasture nearest the house. I bellowed "Mooooo," trying to get them to look up, but they just lay there staring into the heat and flicking flies with their tails. Grandma Margaret had delivered the cows one afternoon in a big red trailer. They'd clomped down the metal ramp and stepped nervously onto foreign grass. Grandma had stood there smiling, hand on hip, counting them as they exited while Mom poured feed and filled the water trough. The cattle were restless and frequently broke loose and ran through the yard. Usually, they made it as far as the road, then lost steam and stood around. Somebody always came to the house when the cows were blocking traffic or eating someone's garden, and Mom would round up whatever help there was and herd them back to the barn. Grandma thought a bull might impose order upon the unruly group, so she'd brought out a brute named Oscar. The cows assimilated Oscar right off, though, and the number of escapes increased.

Standing on the roof, I noticed that the sky was flawlessly, abysmally blue and fixed with white puffy clouds that looked like the clouds on the cover of a church bulletin I'd seen. A woman who lived down the road had taken me to a service. During the long sermon, the minister talked pleasantly about angels. They sounded wonderful, better than people; they had harps and wings and didn't have to worry. I asked the woman about them on the way back to the farm. She explained that people became angels when they ascended to heaven, which was a perfect place in the sky. Becoming an angel seemed to me the best anyone could hope for, floating up into the endless blue. I asked Nick if he'd like to become an angel. He said yes.

We were holding hands at the roof's edge when Mom came around the corner with a basket of laundry. She looked like a stick woman.

"Mom," I yelled, "we're going to be angels!"

My mother glanced around and up and, upon seeing us, dropped the basket of laundry. She stuck out one hand as if stopping traffic and ran off sideways. "You kids stay right there!" she yelled. "*Don't* move!" She disappeared into the house. Next thing I knew, Mom's face was in the open window. Then came her arms, then her whole body. She grabbed me and Nick by the backs of our shirts and dragged us into the attic. "Are you trying to give me a heart attack? You are *not* to play up here anymore!" Her face was red. I saw that she was shaking.

We sat at the bottom of the oak staircase, chins in hands, as

Mom marched up with a screwdriver and removed the brown enamel doorknobs from both doors that led to the attic. She marched back down, past us, with the knobs in the pocket of her shorts. They clacked together as she hurried silently outside.

Dad wasn't home that day. For reasons yet unclear to me, he came home less and less often as the months passed. It got so his returns felt like visits, his departures shadows that kept his place at the kitchen table. By winter, he'd all but abandoned us. I remember seeing my father only twice after the snow covered the ground. One time, he and Uncle Tom showed up with a snowmobile and a sled shaped like a disc. Mom bundled us in thick coats, scarves, mittens, and boots with plastic bags inside, and Dad and Tom pulled us across Lake Sylvia on the sled. They shot us over snowdrifts and we flew into the air, landing with a thud on the ice. We laughed so hard tears welled up and frosted our eyelashes. I thought we were having a wonderful time until Dad looked back at me from the driver's seat and forced a sad, scrunched smile.

The other time we saw him was Christmas Eve. The house was decorated with the Santas and snowflakes Nick and I had cut from construction paper. The plastic tree, set up at the foot of the staircase, was covered with red balls and tinsel. My brother and I lay in bed, sleeping fitfully, anticipating reindeer patter. We woke to a loud bang at the door and Mom speaking in an angry tone. "Where in the hell have you been?" It was Dad's voice that answered, but it sounded cold, unfamiliar. "None of your goddamned business! Can't you just leave it alone?" There was more loud talk and then a messy crash. My brother and I ran out into the upstairs hallway. We saw the Christmas tree, upended and shimmering against the staircase. Red ornaments rolled down the steps, tapping *plink, plink, plink, plink*. Dad looked up and gave another awful, scrunched smile. He accused our dog Sandy of knocking over the tree. Nick, in his brown-and-red cowboy pajamas, ran up to Sandy and yelled in her face, "Bad dog! Bad dog!"

Days and weeks and months on the farm were defined by Dad's

absence. The phone rarely rang. When it did, Mom used her explaining voice. "He's not here. No, I don't know. I'll tell him. I said I'd tell him." Or, "He's not here. No, I don't know. Unfortunately, we have no way to pay that. If you must." Dad had stopped paying the bills. The hardware store demanded reimbursement for the building supplies. The gas company refused to fill the drum that fed our furnace. One night I turned on the faucet to brush my teeth and nothing came out. The well had run dry just when the ground was too frozen to dig a new one. All we had to separate our home from a cave was electricity. It was illegal to shut off someone's power in the dead of winter.

Mom gathered buckets of snow and melted them on the yellow electric Sears stove to make water. She left the oven on for heat, the door propped open and surrounded by a barricade of chairs. She trolled the yard in the bitter cold with a red wagon, gathering piles of sticks to keep the fireplace roaring. Sometimes we roasted hot dogs or marshmallows in the living room; it made the fire seem cozy, by choice. At night, the four of us slept huddled together in one bedroom with an electric heater under Liz's crib. Mom slept on the floor between the beds occupied by my brother and me. She wedged a chair under the doorknob for security. There were chairs wedged against most of the doors in the house because the locks were broken. The doorjambs were loose and splintered from loud crashes and angry voices.

"Mom?"

"Yes."

"Are we safe?"

Mom rose to her knees in the dark. She leaned over and pulled me to her chest. "Don't you worry. Nobody is going to come in here and touch you kids. I'd be just like a mother lion. Nothing is as fierce as a mother lion."

Our only regular visitor was Dad's mom, Grandma Margaret. She showed up at the farm each week bearing a carload of supplies—potatoes, meat, milk, eggs, marshmallows. She always brought a case of beer and a bottle of vodka for Mom. The two would share a few drinks in the living room and talk in low tones. Mom would even laugh sometimes. Then Grandma would drive off and we'd be alone again.

The booze Grandma brought served as Mom's tonic for getting through the days and nights. She fell into a stupor, so that sometimes you'd ask a question and she wouldn't hear. The kitchen table was her podium. She sat there for hours, entranced, gazing out the window toward the garage that housed the blue Plymouth. Dad had taken the license plates off so Mom wouldn't drive away. If she was planning something, she never mentioned it. She kept us fed and warm, but she'd disappeared.

Spring arrived with green buds that shoved their way up through the earth and purple storms that swept across our property. The air would fall completely still, charged with an eerie green cast. Then would come the escalating gusts of wind. The windows would rattle and small items would roll by as we stood watching: branches, paper plates, tufts of cow hair. Finally, as if the momentum were too great to withstand, the sky would open up with torrents of rain. Spidery lightning bolts would flash, followed by thunder that sounded like splitting wood.

One afternoon, I awoke to find Mom rustling through our dresser, cramming handfuls of clothing into paper grocery bags. Her hair was combed flat and wet against her head.

"Mom, what are you doing?"

"Let's get up, we're going for a drive."

"Where?"

"We're leaving. We're going to stay with Mugs and Bernie."

"How come?"

"I'll explain later. Let's get up and get dressed. Help your brother get dressed."

Mom finished filling the bags with our most portable belongings—clothes, toys, photographs. Then she herded us down the grand staircase. My aunt Mugs and uncle Bernie, along with Grandma Bernice, Mom's mom, stood on the landing. They tried to sound upbeat.

"We think you should come home for a while," they said.

The four of them grabbed armfuls of bags and rushed in and out the front door, loading the back of the Plymouth, which Bernie said he'd drive, plates or no. "Let a cop pull me over," he said. "See what he thinks about all this." We headed down the driveway, away from the farm, me and Nick in the backseat surrounded by pants and shirts and blankets. I examined the house and trees through the car window. I'd just built a home out of sand for the ants that lived in our driveway. I worried that the ant cave would get crushed, that a car would drive over it because I wouldn't be there to direct traffic.

Mom turned around from the front seat and told us everything would be okay. She was holding a lit cigarette close to her face. She looked scared, but I believed her.

4

The new house had brown shag carpeting

WE ARRIVED IN WATERTOWN, South Dakota, in the blind dark with a pile of worn bedding and empty pockets. We parked at the curb next to Mugs and Bernie's house, just behind their truck and camper. Exhausted, we lugged what we could inside, moving silently and slowly as if something crucial had been kicked from our middles. Mugs, round-faced and kind, fixed a plate of peanut butter and jelly sandwiches and worked some quick logistics. She divided us among the bedrooms of my four cousins. Mugs and Bernie weren't rich. The small rooms were crowded. But their home was warm and messy. I decided that it was much better to have too many people in a house than too few.

For months, we subsisted under my aunt and uncle's protective wing. We wore our cousins' hand-me-down clothes, some of which Mugs sewed from scratch, and camped with their family at Lake Kampeska in the camper, which made us feel like we were flying when we rode in the narrow space above the truck cab. Mom remained demoralized. During conversations, her eyes tended to slide off the person she was talking to and fix on the wall. She moped and wondered, occasionally out loud, what kind of idiot she must have been to have chosen a man like Dad, and then to have stayed with him for so long. Yet she had to find a way to move on, land a decent job, and start paying bills, to somehow feel good again and reclaim the big ideas she'd harbored as a girl.

Mom and her five siblings hailed from a podunk town in southern Minnesota. Her family was ragged poor, due to a stubborn romantic streak. Grandma Bernice came from money, but she fell in love with a man her family abominated. When she married him anyway, she was cut off without a cent. Grandpa, nicknamed Slim, possessed charm and skill. Legend has it he could lay his hand on any engine and immediately diagnose what was wrong with it. One time, the well-worn story goes, a plane managed an emergency landing in a cornfield near town. The locals woke Slim in the middle of the night and hauled his union-suited ass to the site, where he supposedly felt the tremors of the ailing motor and, like a minister healing a crippled man, fixed the problem in minutes.

Slim was also a shitheel. He fathered six children then ran off, only to show up now and again with such impractical gifts as parakeets. (Mom swears had the birds been larger, Grandma would have cooked them for dinner.) He couldn't even keep the kids' names straight. Bernice, for her part, was sturdy and good. She threw her strong back into supporting her children by scrubbing floors, cooking Sunday dinners for wealthy folks, and working other people's farms.

Mom's family lived at the bottom of a hill in a house that flooded each spring. The place offered few conveniences; there was no flushing toilet. It was so small that some of the children had to sleep outside in a lean-to. (Later, one of Grandma's brothers would slip her enough money to buy the bigger, dryer place at the top of that same hill.) At least they never went hungry. The yard featured a couple of reliable apple trees and Grandma always had a bucket of lard around, remuneration for helping local farmers render their meat. The family maintained a steady diet of apple dumplings, sugar-coated popcorn, and bread dipped in grease. The kids wore used clothing, which Bernice deftly repaired: she'd take all the stitching out of an old jacket, turn it inside out so the good fabric showed, and sew it back together again. Presto.

Mom was a middle child, born in July 1941. She grew up healthy and feisty, playing in ditches with cardboard boxes and broken kitchen utensils. She tended to ally herself with underdogs and didn't mind a fight. Once, in grade school, Mom happened upon a group of boys who'd thrown her sister Evie's sweater up into a tree. Evie was slow. She'd been held back a few grades and so was more developed than the other girls. She jumped up and down trying to reach the sweater while the boys ogled her chest. Mom chased the boys away with balled fists, threatening to beat the crap out of them all.

Grandma Bernice's kids worked. Mom was no exception. When she was fourteen, she took a waitressing job in the cafe where Grandma cooked. Grandma instructed Mom to lie about her age in order to get hired. It was the only time she ever told Mom to lie. When you're poor, people critique you mercilessly. They expect you to cheat, so you have to guard your honor, stand by your word. That was Grandma's philosophy, anyway. It's my mother's too. If you trace Mom's lineage back far enough, you come to Abe Lincoln. Honest Abe.

One afternoon at the cafe, a tall, husky man in a cowboy hat sauntered through the door and settled at the counter. Mom poured hot coffee into a white ceramic mug and moved on to another customer. Bernice pulled Mom aside. She asked, "Do you know who that is?" Mom said she didn't. "That's your dad." Bernice tried to introduce Mom to Slim, but Mom didn't want any part of it. Slim was the bad guy, the one who'd run off. If he didn't give a shit, why should she? Mom saw her father again late one night when he showed up at the house with a carton of ice cream. The family didn't have a refrigerator, so Bernice rousted all her children from bed and they passed the ice cream around until it was gone. Grandma didn't eat any, claiming to dislike ice cream. Later that night, Mom walked into the kitchen and found her scraping out the inside of the container, sopping up the remains with a piece of stale bread.

Mom was popular at school and beautiful—slender, with big dark blue eyes and chestnut hair—maybe even a little haughty. Her family called her "princess" because she pressed her skirts with sugar water and pin-curled her hair each night. The local boys tried to win Mom's heart, but she had ambitious dreams, maybe of becoming a nurse, certainly of abandoning jerkwater farm country. She was elected the school's homecoming queen in 1959 and was stunning the night of the prom, donning rhinestones around her neck and a gossamer chiffon dress. For a graduation present, Grandma Bernice gave Mom a white cardboard suitcase. Mom packed it and hauled it to Minneapolis.

Like so many small-town refugees before her, my mother moved into an apartment building on the city's south side. She and her roommates laughed and flirted and went to parties. One night, Mom's roommate came home all moon-eyed, talking about this great guy she'd met. He was intelligent and flat-out gorgeous. He really seemed to be going places, she said. His name was John Vogel.

Dad dropped by the apartment one night to pick up the room-mate for a date. Mom's hair was rolled up tight in curlers and covered with a white kitchen towel that was knotted in front. My father introduced himself, looking her right in the eyes. He cracked a couple of understated jokes and Mom laughed. That was the initial attraction. The roommate eventually found somebody else, somebody she married, and Dad asked if Mom might like to go out.

The two took a lot of walks together, talking incessantly. Some things were immediately evident about my father. He had big ideas, seemed to know exactly what he wanted and how to get it. He was smart and sophisticated, even sort of glamorous: early in their relationship, he took Mom to his aunt Florence's funeral, where she described the guests as "all looking like movie stars." Dad couldn't have been more different from Grandma Bernice and the house with no toilet.

Yet now, twelve years later, it looked as though Mom had pistol-shot her mother's life right in the bull's-eye. She was stranded in a small town, separated from a no-account husband, and saddled with a pack of young hungry kids. She was starting from less than zero. She would have to scratch and crawl to get out of Dad's big, deep footprint.

When I asked Mom whether Dad would ever live with us again—it seemed to me I should have a father around—she said, simply, "No." I asked why not. "There are things about him you don't know, things I'll tell you about when you get older." I pestered her often for this information, always drawing the same cryptic response. Then, one morning, she was sitting in front of a small mirror propped on an upside-down ice cream bucket applying blue eye shadow. She was wearing long, orange-striped pajamas and sipping a cup of black coffee as the radio played: Helen Reddy, Tony Orlando and Dawn, then Carly Simon's "You're So Vain." Mom stopped brushing her eyelids at the melody's first notes. She cracked a wicked half smile and looked over at me as I heaped teaspoons of sugar onto my Honeycombs. "Listen to this song," she said. "This song could have been written about your dad." I followed the words carefully, the part about walking into a party as if walking onto a yacht and having one eye in the mirror. Dad is pretty good-looking, I thought. Nothing really wrong with that. Then came the line, *Well you're where you should be all of the time, and when you're not you're with some underworld spy or the wife of a close friend.* "Especially that part," Mom said. "That's your dad to a T."

Each Sunday, Mom spread open the newspaper and circled job descriptions with a pen. She wasn't entering the workforce for the first time—she'd been employed by the cafe; a hospital; and FC Hayer in Minneapolis, a distributor of household appliances. "I can do anything if given the chance," she declared to the ink and paper. "Just look at all the people out there with good jobs who don't know siccum." Mom primped for interviews, slipping her shapely frame into earth-toned polyester pantsuits and heels. She stood before the hall mirror examining herself. She stuck her fingers into her hair and fluffed. Her assessment was always that she looked "a fright."

She didn't look a fright, though. She looked beautiful. Back then, other kids were always asking me, that's your *mother*?

One afternoon, Mom came home with a bag of donuts. She'd landed a position as bookkeeper for a minor food wholesaling operation. When she introduced us to Jack, the short, blockish man who owned the company, he laid his hairy hand on Mom's shoulder and smiled wetly. I flashed on Mom the way men saw her: pretty, smart, and irresistibly desperate. She stood with Jack, uncomfortable but in no position to say so, and announced gaily, "Kids, this is my new boss!" A job was a job. A paycheck meant we could move into our own place, which we did, though we didn't move far. We rented the Band-Aid-colored, stucco, two-bedroom house next door to Mugs and Bernie's. Despite the fact that it was the early seventies and the National Organization for Women was in high gear and the Equal Rights Amendment had been passed by Congress, Mom couldn't get heat or electricity without Bernie's cosignature. She was bearing the responsibilities of both father and mother, yet the goddamned city wouldn't give her heat.

Mom worked and grocery shopped and furnished our house with garage sale tables and thrift store lamps. She moved forward, but not quickly enough. Evenings, she came home depressed. She slipped past us playing in the yard and plunked down at the kitchen table with a plastic iced-tea glass full of vodka poured from the bottles she kept under the sink.

It was due to Mom's gulping thirst for vodka that I first saw Johnny Carson. Nick, Liz, our cousins, and I had been terrorizing the block, banging on neighbors' doors and running away. Mugs corralled her kids inside, so we headed home too. When we got there, Mom was lying fully clothed on the living room sofa. Her face was shiny with sweat and she snored and moaned, muttering occasionally. I flipped on the television. We sat on the floor with our backs to Mom until sunlight faded entirely from the room and Liz dozed off. Nick, who'd bathroom-trained Liz without much assistance, slid her into the lower bunk in our bedroom, then climbed into the upper bed and went to sleep himself. I stayed up. I changed into my long blue pajamas with the lace collar and concocted one of my special drinks, which consisted of Tang and canned fruit cocktail. When Carson's monologue came on, I giggled out loud. I considered myself genuinely lucky because I got to watch whatever I wanted for as long as I wanted while all the other first graders were in bed. I glanced back at Mom, wanting her to wake and catch me, to commemorate my daring. I kicked the TV stand into the wall, but she didn't budge. I stepped outside onto the grass and looked up and down the street. It was a weeknight and most of the houses were dark. I stared down at Mom, her face pressed into the rough fabric of the sofa, and pulled off her work shoes. Then I crawled into bed with Liz.

A few days or weeks or months later, the three of us were asleep in our room when we were startled awake by Mom's bellowing. Before we could do or say anything, the bedroom door flung open and the overhead light flashed, harsh and bright. I could see that Bernie and Mugs were hauling Mom through the living room by her arms and legs, much the way lifeguards drag drowning people from lakes. Like most drowning people, Mom was kicking and twisting her body to get away. Then, somehow, Dad appeared. He was bent down, looking into our faces.

We hadn't seen much of Dad since leaving the farm, and his presence added urgency to the situation. I begged for details, but he acted agitated and sour. He said, "I need you to get out of bed and get dressed, okay? As fast as you can."

The three of us did as asked, while he snatched up piles of tiny underwear and shirts and pants. He ushered us into the backseat of his car.

"Where are we going?"

"You're coming to live with me in Minneapolis. Your mother will be in the hospital for a while." My father lit a cigarette and sucked a few quick puffs. His tone swooped from high and exasperated to a low growl. "I've had it with her. I really have. Drinking night and day and passing out. It's disgusting."

I couldn't decide whether we were being rescued or kidnapped. "Did Mom say it was okay to take us like this?"

"She's so out of it, she doesn't know what in the hell is going on."

"Will we ever see her again?"

Dad's shoulders lowered and his voice mellowed, as if he'd considered Nick, Liz, and me thinking people for the first time. "Sure. Oh, sure you will. We'll visit."

I didn't say anything more. The three of us sat close together in the backseat, riding along the highway in the dark as globs of headlight floated past like colossal fireflies. Then, just as we reached the Minnesota border, Dad abruptly turned the car around. "Maybe this wasn't such a good idea after all," he said. He dropped us back in Watertown with a piece of paper on which he'd scribbled his phone number.

Mom recovered. She returned to us lighter and happier, her eyes clear and focused. Occasionally, she broke into little dance steps, clicking her tongue to some internal melody and kicking her leg out to the side. She hung a wooden plaque printed with the Serenity Prayer over the dresser in her room. I sat on the bed watching her straighten it. "What's that?" I asked. She said, "It's a smart way to live." Then she read it aloud. "God grant me the serenity to accept the things I cannot change, courage to change the things I can, and wisdom to know the difference." Ah, I thought, so that's what's been the problem. Not enough wisdom to know the difference. Mom was unabashed about having been through treatment. She was proud she'd made it. She even drove me past the clinic. "That's it there," she said, pointing with a cigarette. "I'm through drinking. Things are going to be much better from now on." Then she stubbed the cigarette out in the ashtray.

One evening after work, Mom was mixing a batch of dreaded elbow noodle, hamburger, and tomato hotdish when she heard pounding in the yard. She walked outside and discovered our landlord applying the finishing touches to a wooden "For Sale" sign. "Not to worry," he chirped. "You don't have to move until I find a buyer." Mom, indignant that she hadn't been warned, informed the cheerful fellow that we would be moving immediately. See how he'd like a couple of months with an empty house and no rent.

We left the Band-Aid bungalow, bumping from rental to rental. There was the house next to the Persons, an old couple who watched us after school. (They were pleasant, but their house smelled of peanut butter and decaying skin.) When the Persons told Mom our landlady was sneaking into our house during the day, Mom did battle again. She phoned, but the landlady didn't bother to be embarrassed. She claimed to be checking up on Mom's housekeeping, which the lease allowed. Again, my mother gave notice on the spot. We moved into an apartment attached to the back of a grocery store, a ramshackle hut with a large, yawning heater grate in the middle of the living room floor that melted the bottoms of our tennis shoes.

Finally, fed up with condescending landlords and addresses that ended in ½, Mom purchased a house in 1976, when I was nine. She was desking at a real estate firm. One of the agents happened across a green three-bedroom with a fern bed under the kitchen window and a basketball hoop. He declared it perfect for my family. Mom said she couldn't afford it, but the agent explained that he'd talked with the firm's owner and the two would contribute their sales commissions toward the down payment. Grandma Bernice advised against the purchase, worried that Mom could lose everything, but Mom didn't have much to lose. She scraped together the balance of the down payment and every payment after that and we didn't move for six years. I've never lived for that long in any one place since.

Mom worked from eight each morning until five, often later and sometimes on weekends. She attended night classes and earned her real estate license. When selling houses didn't bring in enough money, she took a job selling insurance. In her brown Chevy Chevette—the first new car she'd ever purchased—Mom traversed the country roads of South Dakota, cold-selling policies to skeptical farmers. Doors slammed and dogs bared their teeth. At the end of each week, the inside of the Chevette was layered with paper and dirt. Sometimes, out of sympathy, I vacuumed the car and spray-shined the windows.

Nick, Liz, and I were left with baby-sitters or on our own. Mostly on our own. Mom scribbled notes with instructions: *Kids! For dinner make Chili Dogs—Hope you did well in Field Day Nick—I'll try to be home early as possible—I'm working near Summit and Waubay.* Because we were so often without Mom, we constantly vied for her attention. We drew pictures and forced her to choose the best. We begged her to watch TV with us. One night, she didn't get home until almost eleven. She pulled up to our corner and spotted a figure crouched under the glowing streetlamp. It was Nick, waiting. He'd been waiting for hours. Mom was mortified. That's when she decided to quit the insurance business and start a wallpapering and painting service with Mugs.

At the beginning of each week, Mom taped a handwritten chore sheet to the front of the refrigerator listing the fee she'd pay for each duty. Washing laundry, which included sitting on the washer during its spin cycle so it didn't scoot across the room, earned 50 cents; making the beds earned 35; feeding our pet squirrel earned a dime; and attaching Buffy, our Lhasa apso, to her leash earned a nickel. By the end of each week, the page was always dominated by my initials, with a handful from Liz. My brother's were nowhere to be found. Mom paid Nick anyway, which I protested wasn't fair.

I was Donna Reed. I dusted and cooked and even collected recipes. I specialized in chocolate chip cookies and meat loaf. Once, after I'd organized and polished the house, Nick came through the door with his friend David. They tracked mud across the carpet and jabbed with a butter knife at the pan of coconut bars I'd baked. Nick laughed when I tried to make them stop. I sobbed and screamed. When I called Mom at work, she told me to calm down.

I'd just started seventh grade, a nightmare. Elementary school had been easy. I'd enjoyed loyal friends. I'd established and been president of the stamp club. My grades were good and teachers adored me. Mom says they always expressed surprise when they learned I was from a "broken home" because I seemed so "well adjusted."

In Watertown, there were a handful of grade schools, but only one junior high. That meant the poor kids from the south side, like me, were lumped in with the rich kids from the north side. The rich kids set the rules. Rigid cliques developed and I stood outside every one. Old friends, deemed to be made of better stuff than I, found acceptance, while I hovered at the fringes (I held the tenuous post of French-braider). I was smart and reasonably pretty, but I cut my own hair and wore garage sale clothing. My pants were either too big or too short and I wore white tube socks with bright orange sneakers.

Dad usually didn't pay the $400 he owed monthly in child support. He spent money on us, but his support was less a constant source of comfort than a sporadic fountain of lavishness. He didn't pay the heat bill; he bought us *things* in order to reap direct and immediate gratitude. When we visited, he took us to fancy malls for clothing and toys. The trips made more glaring our impoverished everyday lives. When I saw wealth up close, when I realized how quickly my social standing improved simply by donning a fashionable outfit, I cursed my terrible luck. Once, Dad bought me a pair of pleated red corduroy pants and a checked blouse with a stylish round collar. After a rich girl publicly fawned over it, I wore the outfit to school three days straight.

If Dad learned we were in need of something significant, he sometimes swept in and tried to save the day. He'd make a grand gesture, then fail to follow through. One of Liz's incisors came in looking like a Dracula fang, so Dad drove her to an orthodontist and had him install braces. Then he didn't pay the bill. When Mom received an angry phone call, she told the dentist he could either yank the braces off or accept the small monthly payments she was able to afford. Years later, after she mailed the last check, the ortho-dontist sent back a note of appreciation.

When my father discovered I wanted to play piano, he bought a brand-new upright and had it delivered to our living room. It was our finest piece of furniture; I polished it fanatically. He signed me up for lessons with a Catholic nun named Sister Mary Margaret, an odd choice given his feelings toward the Church. When I didn't learn the dull songs she assigned (she pushed Bach and Haydn, while I preferred "Music Box Dancer" and "The Sting"), the old and crabby Mary Margaret dropped to her knees and wailed to God: "Please make Jennifer a better child! Please make her learn her lessons!" When I did well, however, all I received was a candy bar. It burned me up that God heard of my failures but not my successes. In the dark, I told God the truth about Mary Margaret. I don't know if God was listening, but Dad stopped sending payments for the lessons. The piano was gone soon after.

Each month began with an empty mailbox and a pointed tirade about the missing child support check, followed by an oration addressing my father's chronic lying. Dad lied consistently, Mom said, and sometimes even "believed his lies," a mental feat beyond the ability of normal people. During their marriage, he'd lied about attending college while Mom earned his tuition. He'd lied about paying rent. He'd lied about other women. The lying was so perva-sive that after a while, Mom didn't know who in the hell Dad was.

I listened. And sometimes I got really angry at my father's bro-ken promises. Mostly, though, I reserved judgment. I was a liar too. At school, I weaved fantastic stories about how my family had lived in Hawaii before moving to South Dakota and how my father was a rich lawyer. I claimed that Mom had been a fashion model and drove a Corvette, though anyone with eyes could see that it was a Chevette. I promised, coolly, that it was only a matter of time before we moved away to California. I hated myself for lying. I knew it was wrong, even potentially disastrous. What's more, I wasn't very good at it. The meanest girls at school responded to my stories by saying,

"That's not true," or "Oh, *really*?" But I couldn't help it: the lies flew from my tongue like spit.

Back then, I believed in God just the way He was described to me, as a stern, bearded man in a high-backed chair aware of every minute detail on earth. I repeatedly fell to my knees and begged for forgiveness, for the exorcism of my inherent badness. The confessing became the punishment.

I'd fled the lunchroom in tears and run all the way home, only to find that everything in our house was wrong. The fake wood paneling was too dark. The muddled brown shag carpeting was matted. The furniture was broken down and webbed with pet hair. Against one wall sat the brown, black, and cream plaid sofa, propped up on phone books because a leg was missing. In front of that was the rectangular coffee table with the veneer chipped off one side, strategically placed so the casual observer wouldn't see the blemish. My neck turned hot. I clenched my teeth and pounded on the sofa with both fists until a thick cloud of dust and hair filled the living room.

From under the sink in the kitchen, I retrieved a pail of Amway cleaning supplies and began scrubbing. I polished surfaces I usually didn't bother with, like the shelf behind the TV that held books on topics such as reincarnation and the small plane that crashed in the Andes, leaving its passengers to eat one another for nourishment. Cradling the bust of the wailing bearded man Dad had sculpted, I polished its eye sockets and lips, and kissed its forehead. I wondered whether I'd be happier living with my father, whether I'd be treated to a stream of gifts and steak dinners. I set the head down and walked to the globe we kept in the corner. I closed my eyes, spun it with the slapping part of my hand, and put my finger down to see where I might live someday. I'd asked fate a question. Did I want to know the answer? I opened my eyes. My finger pointed toward India. I didn't know much about India. At least it wasn't South Dakota.

There was no one else home, except our absurd array of pets. Mom rescued every injured animal she came upon: cats, birds, a baby squirrel she'd spotted lying in the rain by the side of the road. She'd tucked the squirrel into a stocking cap and built a chicken-wire cage in the storage room. I felt ashamed. Were we goddamned hillbillies? Why were we like this? There must be something Mom wasn't telling. I got the idea to hunt for clues in her bedroom. I opened her jewelry box, fingered the large metal owl necklace I sometimes wore like a Wonder Woman breastplate. I opened her dresser drawers and ran my hand along the backs. Then I lifted the edge of Mom's orange brocade bedspread with the cracked foam backing and laid my face on the carpeting so I could see underneath. That's where I found the box.

It was an old carameled-apple box printed with "Tricks or Treats" in orange lettering and a black silhouette of a witch riding a broom. I sat where nobody could spot me and flipped open the lid. Inside was a trove of papers and pictures I'd never seen. There was an early photo of Mom in blue jeans with her girlfriends, grinning and smoking cigarettes. There was another of Mom at homecoming, standing with a blond boy at the top of a set of bleachers, wearing a big tinfoil star on her head. I dug deeper and found some shots of Dad. These I examined very closely. In one, he's slouched back on a patterned sofa wearing a cardigan and a plaid hat tilted forward in comic fashion; a freshly lit cigarette dangles from his mouth. In another, he's stepping from a rowboat in which a man and woman sit. He's wearing Ray-Ban sunglasses and black socks with white pants. The caption on the back reads, *Our cabin on Browns Lake.* Then I came upon the most stunning photo of all: Mom and Dad are standing arm in arm on a city street, Dad in a brown suit and thin tie and Mom in heels and a fitted dress that falls just below the knee. Their hairdos are perfect. On the back, Mom wrote, *John & Me—Wedding day. October 20, 1962.* I peered at their faces. They look proud, pleased with themselves. In love.

At the bottom of the box was a small stack of letters, all from

Dad. I couldn't help reading them. My father was a mystery and this was a bona fide excavation. He used his sweetest voice in the letters. He apologized for what had happened, though, to my consternation, he didn't go into useful detail. He promised to be a better man if only Mom would come home. He said he was so lonely that he might kill himself. When I saw how persuasive Dad could be, I realized Mom must have had good reason for leaving and not going back. I admired her fortitude.

I couldn't mention the letters or the pictures to Mom, though they lit up my head like electricity. I wouldn't be able to sleep that night, but then I didn't sleep much most nights. Lying awake, I watched the numbers flip over on my Sears clock radio. It made tiny grinding noises as the tension built behind each new number and let out a little click as each number fell into place. I thought about Mom and Dad and school and who I was turning out to be. I wished that a strong, handsome man would break in through the window and rescue me. I arched my back over the edge of the bed so that my head was upside down and imagined the floor was the ceiling and the ceiling the floor. I stared at the door, trying to shut it by sheer will. I was sure the only reason the door didn't budge was that I didn't truly believe it would. My doubts were all that stood in the way.

Mom called from her room, "Girls, sing 'The Rose.'" Liz and I hated it when Mom asked us to sing "The Rose." We rolled our eyes, but did our best to stay in tune. We harmonized from the top, "Some say love, it is a river that drowns the tender reed." Mom listened in the dark, curled up in her bed, atop the carameled-apple box like a bird on a precious egg.

My father really knew how to live

5

"**D**AD, IS A CADILLAC expensive?" We were driving up State Highway 10 toward Brainerd in the mint green DeVille. Nick and Liz were fussing in back. I was riding shotgun. The trunk was brimming with luggage.

"Nooo. Huh-uh. They used to be. But now, because of the oil shortage, people can't give away these big gas guzzlers."

"That's not what Mom says."

"I'll bet your mother's Chevette cost more than this car. She bought that new, right? Well, I bought this used. It hardly cost anything. The demand for Cadillacs is way down." Dad placed an unlit cigarette in his mouth and spun it slowly with his fingers. Crystal Gayle crooned ". . . but don't it make my brown eyes blu-u-u-ue" in the background. The tape had looped through twice already. Dad had a thing for womany women, the kind with soft hands and dreamy eyes. The following year, when Victoria Principal would debut as Pam Ewing on the TV show *Dallas*, Dad would develop a whopping crush, describing her as "classy."

I lifted my hand from my right knee, where I kept it to mask a nubby wart, and pushed the button that lowered the window. The terrain was familiar. We'd traveled this route at the beginning of each summer three years running, since I was eight. First came the Dairy Queen outside Clear Lake, where we stopped for Peanut Buster Parfaits and chili dogs. Then came a boring string of small towns—Rice, Royalton, Little Falls—and endless fields of young corn striving for knee high by the Fourth of July.

The trip's progress was measured by the approach of three landmarks: the nuclear power plant with its slender stacks, booming Fort Ripley, and the Minnesota state prison at St. Cloud, which abutted the highway and stood in stark contrast to the leafy surroundings. The prison was enclosed by an imposing granite wall, so high and gray and smooth that it was difficult to bring into focus. At each corner stood a massive turret that housed a sharpshooting guard, ready to blast anything that moved.

We passed on the right.

"God, Dad, look at that place. Do you think anyone has ever escaped from there?" I had recently watched *Cool Hand Luke,* in which Paul Newman escapes again and again, refusing to let the prison break his spirit.

"Hmmm. I doubt it. You'd have to be a pretty good climber. Besides, the guards would probably catch anyone who tried to make a run for it."

"God." I considered this for a moment. "What do you think it's like in there?" I pictured sweaty Newman with a shovel, and the "box," where guards with grudges locked rule-breaking prisoners.

"I don't know, honey. I imagine it's full of walls. Lots of walls. And noise."

As the prison faded from sight, I watched through the back window. I scoured the ditches, looking for men in blue shirts and striped pants who'd flung themselves over the wall.

By the time we crossed into Brainerd, it was two o'clock in the afternoon. The town was in full summer mode. Boat shops advertised incredible deals via gaudy, primary-colored streamers and signs with exclamation points. Gas stations featured illuminated bait refrigerators stocked with live leeches and earthworms. Everywhere, men in straw hats and baseball caps escorted tanned women and running, rowdy children. Arriving in Brainerd felt like inhaling and exhaling at once, like floating on a warm puff of air. Dad looked over at me and I could see by the way he smirked that he felt it too, the utter lack of responsibility engendered by lake culture. Nobody here was expected to get anything done.

We pulled up to a stoplight in the middle of town, next to a drinking fountain shaped like a lion. In order to take a sip, you had to stick your head into the lion's mouth.

"Look at that." Dad pointed. "You want me to pull over so you can get a drink?"

"Nah. I'd rather keep going, get to the cabin."

Clearly disappointed, he lifted his chin and looked into the backseat via the rearview mirror. "What do you say? Either of you *dare* to stick your head into the lion's mouth for a drink of water?"

Nick and Liz didn't want to either. We'd fake-tempted the lion before. It'd been a long drive.

Dad adored roadside attractions. He'd take us anywhere we wanted, for as long as we wanted. We spent entire days at amusement parks, riding the bumper cars and eating crispy, drippy corn dogs. The first time he escorted us to Paul Bunyan Land—the centerpiece and theme for the entire Brainerd lakes area—he slipped our names to the man in the booth, who piped his voice out to the enormous Paul Bunyan statue. "Hello, Jennifer, Nick, and Liz!" the towering statue bellowed, eyes crazed. The outburst scared the hell out of us, which amused Dad. He loved unexpected moments that superseded the humdrum of everyday life. Dad was the type to order birthday cakes in restaurants, to discreetly corral the staff into standing at our table and singing "Happy Birthday," loudly filling in the blank with one of our names.

Sometimes he tried too hard. Faint panic lurked behind these gay efforts as Dad weighed each individual moment to determine whether he'd won or lost us. He always wanted everything to be perfect, for us to have the best time ever, so that the glow would last into the winter months when he wasn't around. We assured Dad that there was no need to arrange anything special, that we had *come to see him*—instinctively, we used those words. But the stream of sideshows continued: Lumbertown, Deer Land, Prairie Village, the Como Zoo, the Minnesota Zoo, the planetarium, the IDS observation deck, Valleyfair, the Nutcracker Fantasy, the Omnitheater, miniature golf, the Jonathan Padelford, the Betty Crocker kitchen tour.

We saw Dad only three or four times a year, on birthdays, at Christmas, and during summers. Mom enjoyed first pick. She usually had us for the actual holiday, whatever it was, and Dad made do with the time after or before. The previous Christmas Eve had been an exception. Dad had unexpectedly arrived at the green house in Watertown. Likely, he'd been lonely. His whole life, the holidays sent him into a funk. We sat in the living room making small talk. Dad was perched on the crippled sofa, chain-smoking and drinking Folgers, while Nick, Liz, and I piled the gifts he'd brought under the artificial tree, which was looped with rope and nailed to the wall so the cats wouldn't knock it over again. Mom and Dad were polite to one another, but the tension was palpable.

Finally, my father suggested that he treat his three rugrats to a movie. Mom said okay so long as we were back early. We rode in the Cadillac to the uptown theater and parked diagonally out front. As we approached the counter, I noticed heavy disappointment wash across the ticket taker's face.

"Um, we're just getting ready to pack it in," the guy explained. "You're the only customers here. Um, it *is* Christmas Eve."

Dad glanced down at us, saw that our hopes were high, then looked back at the young man. "I know," my father said. "I don't blame you for wanting to get home to your family. But I don't get to see the kids very often. See, they live with their mother." He put his arms around our shoulders like a goose sheltering her young. "This is it for me. I have to head back to Minneapolis tonight."

In this duel of pathos, the guy knew he'd lost. He sold us the tickets and some popcorn that greased through the bag. We sat in the dark on Christmas Eve, all alone in the theater, watching *Rocky*.

Now, with Crystal Gayle still oozing from the stereo, we turned onto Nashway Road, the wooded two-lane that encircles Round Lake. Many of the cabins that surrounded ours were marked with signs. Some offered split wood or fresh bait. Others announced the residing families: "The Johnsons," "The Schneiders," "The Lindvall's!" The plaques were ornate, shaped like flopping walleyes or speedboats, burned with cursive lettering that ended in lassos. Our place had no sign.

We parked in the driveway, near the row of trees we'd planted the previous summer—one for me, one for Nick, one for Liz. They'd grown. Having my very own tree to measure provided a tangible connection to the cabin. The beautiful, breezy lake place was mine, ours. Dad had always called it that, "our" cabin. I shoved the mammoth car door open and leapt out. Nick and Liz sprung the seat forward and did the same. My father stood with his arms straight up, fists balled, stretching his shoulders and neck. "Hey, why don't you slip into your suits and go for a dip?" I was way ahead of him. It was hot, and Round Lake, with its sandy bottom and few weeds, was perfect for swimming.

Originally, when my father purchased the Round Lake property, it featured an older, more rustic cabin that was all raw wood inside. The floors were linoleum; a row of screened windows faced the lake. There was a shellacked picnic table in the dining room. Dad hadn't seemed at home there. On our first night, he foraged through the kitchen looking for something to cook. He found two cans of Campbell's Chunky soup, vegetable beef and chicken dumpling, and mixed them together in a saucepan. Nick set his spoon down and complained that the amalgamation tasted terrible. Dad's eyes narrowed. He growled that it was soup or nothing, so we ate it. That was the only summer we spent at the old cabin. A few months later, it burned down.

Dad built a new, modern structure out of the ashes. It was two stories tall with an attractive dropped roofline and a large, high deck in back. It had white walls and plush carpeting throughout, two fireplaces, and, in the basement, a fully functional bar. The place was tastefully furnished with wicker and glass tables and shelves, hand-constructed by Uncle Tom. Near one of the windows stood a marble chess board. My father had designed the floorplan and done much of the construction himself. He was extremely handy and looked most natural curled over a piece of wood with a hammer, paint flecks and sawdust stuck to his arms.

That fire had destroyed the first cabin, paving the way for my father to build precisely the summer home he'd desired, was no accident. Even as a girl, I knew that. It had been obvious in the way Dad had described the blaze, with detachment bordering on delight. When I'd asked Mom about it, she'd provided unequivocal confirmation: "If that cabin burned down, dollars to donuts your dad burned it down." It had happened before.

Fire struck a cabin Mom and Dad purchased early in their marriage, the one on Browns Lake I'd found a snapshot of in the carameled-apple box. The two had spent an entire summer repairing the bare-bones structure and furnishing it with all the trappings of a romantic hideaway. Then, in the middle of the night, just after Dad had returned to Minneapolis from the lake, the phone rang. It was a neighbor informing Mom that the cabin was now a pile of ash. She was devastated; Dad was nonchalant. It turned out he'd planned the fire from the beginning, making the repairs and even leaving a prized set of golf clubs inside so he'd appear authentically distraught when the police showed up.

Next came a drive-in restaurant. During the year we lived on the Annandale farm, my father built a burger joint. The trouble was, a competing drive-in existed just a few miles down the road. When Dad had difficulty drawing enough business to make a go of it, he paid a late-night visit to the other drive-in, setting the place ablaze by wedging a lit cigarette into a pack of matches. By the time the cigarette smoldered to where it lit the matches, he was long gone.

I wasn't offended by my father's penchant for arson. It made sense, like reading a map. Dad was a renegade, a man who lived by his own rules. He had something on everyone else and I admired him for it. At home, with Mom, there was so much to do, so much toil, just to keep our little barrel from going over the falls. Dad, on the other hand, valued leisure. It seemed to me that he separated his worries from the way in which he moved through the world. He shot me knowing looks and told me I was special and wrapped me in his long, muscular arms. This was how he successfully blurred the line: My father was neither as good nor as bad as people suspected. I loved him and I loved the big, beautiful cabin. The manner in which he'd acquired it was not my concern. It wasn't as though he'd hurt anybody—just some insurance company, and Mom had talked enough about them for me to know they weren't on my side anyway.

As we lugged our bags across the new tar driveway, mushy from the heat, Debbie opened the yellow front door. She stepped out, tall and lanky, her dark red hair tied back in a ponytail. She wore khaki shorts and a green T-shirt with no bra. Her freckled cheeks were pushed into balls, making way for a broad smile. Debbie was Dad's girlfriend. She'd been Dad's girlfriend ever since he and Mom had split, since a little before, actually. They'd both been agents at the real estate firm where my father worked after moving us to the farm. Debbie was eccentric. She wore outrageous hand-sewn outfits, like pink leather skirt-and-jacket sets, and long false eyelashes. She thought Dad the best-looking man she'd ever seen. The two, accompanied by an old drunk who also worked at the firm, started off with lunch. Lunch turned into drinks. Drinks turned into entire afternoons. Entire afternoons turned into my father abandoning us at the farm.

At first, I resented Debbie out of loyalty to Mom. She was the other woman, the whore, the homewrecker. But harsh feelings were difficult to maintain. Debbie wasn't conniving. She was nice and entirely romantic—in the parlance of the time, a free spirit. She looked for the best in people, sometimes even when there wasn't any best to find. She encouraged Dad's mellow side and they fed each other's artistic abilities. The summer prior, she'd led us in the construction of a red, blue, and yellow wooden sun. We'd nailed it to the front of the boathouse, a rustic remnant of the previous cabin.

I placed my mammoth blue suitcase on the floor of the room I shared with Liz. I opened it and arranged a few items on the nightstand: the prized Black Hills gold ring Mom had given me, a box of green, personalized stationery. I unpacked my clothes into the dresser and stowed the suitcase out of sight in the closet. I probably would have turned down the bedcover and placed a mint on my pillow had Dad not come by to stop me. "There is plenty of time to unpack later," he said. "You don't have to do it all now."

Obsessive. Impatient. My father recognized the traits because, inside, he was the same way—always searching for the next thing, sacrificing the present for worry of the future. When he'd hand me a camera, I'd be back in five minutes, all the pictures snapped. He made a point of hiding any activities he'd planned for the day because if I found them out, I became an insufferable pest. *When are we leaving? When are we leaving? When are we leaving?* Dad would shake his head and mumble to Debbie, "I hope she learns to enjoy the moment and doesn't wind up like me."

By 8 p.m., we hadn't eaten dinner. My father was concocting his specialty, bell pepper steak. He claimed it needed to marinate just a bit longer. He'd been claiming that since six. At Dad's, very little happened on schedule. Especially meals, which he felt were more about flavor and conversation than the utilitarian stuffing of faces. Of course, it didn't matter what time we ate or retired to bed because he never worked during summers, save for a day or two when he'd go away on mysterious business. "I think my ship is about to come in," he'd say with a wink, then drive off in the Cadillac.

Dad and Debbie were nearing the end of a second bottle of Liebfraumilch, which he'd explained means "milk of the Blessed Virgin" in German. They sat side by side on yellow deck chairs, discussing improvements to the cabin and various wildlife sightings. A family of chipmunks lived among the shrubs on our property. They were tame. If you clucked your tongue just so and proffered the right bait—usually an orange slice or peanut—they'd tiptoe within five or so feet of you.

"Look at that!" A chipmunk was running the railing toward Dad, who held a chunk of cracker. "He's going to come right up and get it. Nobody move!" But the chipmunk stopped and turned and Dad was forced to toss the cracker into neutral territory.

"You know, we should get some baby ducks." My father leaned toward the doorway and said it again, louder.

Then he turned to Debbie. "Let's see if we can't find some baby ducks."

Music was playing—light, fluttering music with a sad edge. It was Chopin. Dad was rhapsodic about the Nocturnes. When he discovered I liked ELO, he sat me down and told me one of his stories. "I've always liked classical music, even as a kid," he began. "All the other kids were nuts about Elvis, but not me. I listened to Chopin." The rest of the tale went like this: Dad was a loner as a child and nobody liked him much, but that was okay since it kept him from getting sucked into popular culture. Because he was ostracized, he enjoyed the freedom to develop tastes far exceeding other people's. My father was trying to impart a lesson about going your own way or making lemonade out of lemons. Or maybe he just wanted me to like Chopin rather than ELO. He hated rock and roll, even orchestrated rock and roll, because it had no grace.

Now it was nine o'clock, three hours past dinnertime. We were so hungry that we resorted to histrionics. We rolled on the floor gripping our stomachs in an agony that was only partially feigned. Finally, Dad got up, cigarette and wineglass in hand, to cook. By candlelight, we ate pepper steak served on shining red glass plates.

For dessert, we had cherries jubilee ("Watch your eyebrows!" Dad exclaimed as he lit the brandy). Dinner like a festival. By the time we'd scooped up the final cherry, Nick, Liz, and I were red-eyed and slumped in our chairs. My father said we looked like three bumps on a log. He herded us off to bed.

Dad and Debbie were skilled hosts. I'd been to a few of their parties, the best of which was a New Year's Eve soiree at the home Uncle Tom shared with his Swedish girlfriend, Katarina. The house itself was elegant and exotic—it had grass wallpaper in the dining room, a brick floor in the kitchen, dark blue walls upstairs, and a breakfast nook with a glass door upon which Debbie had etched "frukost." The party put the house to its best use. We decorated with candles and lamps that radiated colorful glows. We arranged hors d'oeuvres and set out bottles of expensive liquor. Before the party, my father took me shopping. He purchased the first pair of high heels I ever wore: brown, open-toed sandals. He often treated me as if I were older than I was. He said I was interesting to talk to. That night, I believed it. I floundered about nibbling meatballs from toothpicks and chatting with guests, exhibiting my fawnish social skills.

Around the Fourth of July, Dad and Debbie threw a weekend bender. It wasn't fancy. Preparations had more to do with comfort than elegance—chairs, hamburger, and bags of lemons for home-made lemonade (to be mixed with vodka, of course). We cleared the refrigerator to make room for beer and white wine, and readied the bedrooms for mass sleeping. We pulled blankets from closets and squished handfuls of small sofa pillows into large pillowcases.

Cars from the city arrived. Big sedans. Vans. A truck with a red minibike in back. (I was told not to ride the motorcycle because I was a girl. Having grown up with a can-do mother, I'd never encountered this argument. I later peeled off on the minibike and nearly collided with a tree.) The guests slid their vehicles into open slots on the grass. Doors slammed. Kids bolted to the lakeshore.

Brown paper bags in hand, grown-ups approached the cabin's yellow door: Tom, stylish Katarina, my aunt Cheryl and her daughters, Debbie's pretty blond sister, an overly tanned wife, a mustachioed husband, a man who laughed whenever his son fell down, another who couldn't stop coughing. Happy young people mixed with worn, shifty people. Wearing his "The Word Is Legs: Help Spread the Word" T-shirt, my father trotted to the driveway with greetings.

Dad stationed himself on the lake bank, just beyond the deck, and began tending a mass of sizzling patties. Party guests in shorts and low-cut sundresses leaned against the wooden rail above. Sophisticates. The people laughed and Dad smirked, thinking up the next wisecrack. Tom broke through the line and tossed a handful of firecrackers into the grill. They exploded with a series of loud pops that sent Dad reeling backward. He threw down the long-handled spatula and ran inside, grabbing a beach towel along the way. The two tore through the house, Tom in the lead and Dad right behind, snapping him on the ass.

My brother, sister, and I were the objects of much curiosity. One of Dad's friends, an older man with a face like raw pot roast, repeatedly cornered us, slurring, "The last time I saw you, you were *this* big." With his hands, he indicated our previous size as approximately the same as a loaf of bread. He handed whichever of us he was talking to a dollar just before we squeezed away. The more he drank, the hazier became his memory. We must have taken in fifteen dollars.

Dad sipped vodka all afternoon, keeping pace with his guests. He was humming happily ("dee-dee-dee") and rummaging through a drawer when I entered the kitchen. "Hey, that looks pretty good." He was commenting on my hair, which I had pasted back with a series of barrettes and bobby pins.

"Yeah, right."

I'd begged Dad to take me to a salon to have my hair professionally feathered. I wanted bangs like Kristy McNichol's. My father didn't spend money on fashion. He wore the same Wrangler cutoffs

and loafers all summer. He owned only a handful of shirts. He purchased us kids generic orange tennis shoes from the Holiday station
store. In fact, he bought everything from the Holiday station store:
fishing poles, inner tubes, towels, groceries. At the same time, he
always chose the small bottle of ketchup, not the economy size,
refusing to invest in the future. Dad proposed cutting my hair himself. How hard could it be? He was very convincing. He sat me down
in the boathouse and went to work. But, instead of cutting my
bangs in layers so they parted neatly back into an inverted V, he literally cut my bangs in the shape of an inverted V. The hairs in the
middle were only centimeters long. I looked ridiculous.

"Awww," he said, scrubbing the top of my head with his fingertips. Then he offered to mix up a conciliatory malt with the malt
maker he'd purchased at a local flea market. It was an antique, with
a heavy chrome head that tilted back and a thick, cloth-covered
cord. It was also in need of repair, occasionally jolting the operator
with an electrical shock. He gathered the malt powder, the ice
cream, and a special malt glass that fluted at the top like a daffodil.
He always ate vanilla malts with just a dash of chocolate. I took
mine the same. He plugged in the machine and a spark of electricity sneaked out from the motor and licked his index finger. "Damn
it!" Dad shook his hand as if drying fingernails. Then he finished
blending the malt.

Always, the days leading up to our departure for Watertown were
torturous. But they were worst in the fall. That's when the sadness
of leaving was compounded by the ritual of readying the cabin for
winter: breaking down the dock, stowing the life jackets, bagging up
the food.

It was quiet in the house as I searched corners and under beds
for that last pair of crumpled shorts. My father appeared in the
doorway. "I sure am going to miss you," he said with tears in his
eyes. "You know, when you kids aren't around, I don't know what to

do with myself. I never go out to eat. I just heat up TV dinners." The image of Dad lonely, sitting with a foiled meal by the X-ray glare of the television, sent me into convulsions. We embraced. Liz joined, also wailing and in tears. Deepening our anguish, Jim Croce's "Time in a Bottle" came on the radio.

I knew that what my father said wasn't true. There were too many glossy matchbooks around with restaurant names on them. But I also knew that he wasn't being cruel. He only wanted us to miss him. That he thought this the only way to ensure we'd miss him made me sadder than the story he'd concocted.

We packed the car with our belongings—more than we'd come with—while Dad double-checked the cabin doors. Dry leaves blew in swirls across the driveway. The lake made a lapping sound, beckoning us to stay.

January 1995

6

IPARKED THE ESCORT in the snow-covered lot down the road from *City Pages* and braved the icy sidewalks in knee-high suede boots. I was thick into reporting a story about the late-night murder of a Minneapolis police officer in a pizza restaurant on Lake Street. The officer was white. The convicted killers were black. The city had become hysterical after the shooting; politicians declared innocence lost while the citizenry double-locked their doors against natives of Detroit, Chicago, and Kansas City. I was sure the wrong men had been sent to prison. For months I'd been pulling the case apart. My cubicle was littered with court transcripts. The phone blinked messages.

Across town, my father was facing his own legal Waterloo. I was too busy defending strangers to know a thing about it.

On Monday, January 16, while I marked documents with a yellow highlighter and debated witness accounts, U.S. Customs agents were rummaging through the box Dad mailed from Brownsville, discovering the cocaine and counterfeiting supplies. A Secret Service agent wearing a delivery-guy outfit was orchestrating a multi-departmental raid on his shop. Dad, faced with a room full of police, was answering yes, this is my counterfeit money; yes, the authentic money in my wallet was derived from counterfeiting; and yes, I will put my wrists together so they can be cuffed. These details

I learned later, through interviews and news accounts and public documents.

Because the court deemed Dad upstanding for a counterfeiter, he was loosed the day after his arrest. There were conditions, of course, like he couldn't leave Minnesota, he had to pee into a cup when asked to, and he would be required to pay $10,000 if he failed to materialize at his next hearing, scheduled for January 23 at 11 A.M. Aside from his being free, the situation was bleak. There wasn't, as my father would have said, a snowball's chance in hell he was going to beat the case. The evidence was irrefutable: photos of his shop, packages of fake money, his confession. Plus, the police had seized everything Dad owned of value, leaving him at the mercy of the public defender's office. Public defenders are practically saints, but they tend to be so overburdened that they can't spend much time investigating or preparing for court. They push plea bargains rather than jury trials. I don't know whether Dad would have opted for a trial, but it's hard to imagine even a plea bargain that would have spared him spending the rest of his life behind bars.

Dad used to say, "Never expect anything and you won't be disappointed." Whenever he said this, I would call him cynical, to which he would reply, "I'm not a cynic, I'm a realist." I suppose that when he stepped from the front door of the jailhouse, he was thinking he'd expected too much. And received nothing. Because no matter how wrongheaded his decisions, Dad usually pinned the blame on other people or on the cockeyed rules of the world. Though he evinced the values of a dead nerve, he was anything but. Dad was the guy who'd been dealt a bum hand. Society owed him, but wouldn't settle up. Who could blame him for taking what he could? Dad's cynicism derived from sentimentality: he'd lost faith in people because people always let him down.

The disappointments were well documented in his stories, his vignettes of anguish, sounding perfectly tuned notes of sorrow. He released them just at the moment they'd achieve maximum impact. He'd summon a shadow monster to the surface on a clear blue day, so that by the time he finished spinning a particular tale, you were distrustful of beauty, suspicious of peace.

Once, when I was eleven, we shuffled in cross-country skis across Gull Lake in Brainerd, breathing ice into our scarves and squinting at the sun. The promised reward was hot chocolate at one of the lakeside lodges. We were inside, mugs in hand, sitting at a small wooden table.

"Boy, my feet just won't warm up." Dad rubbed each furiously with the palms of his hands as if attempting to spark a fire. He wore layered pairs of nylon dress socks, the outermost of which bore light blue stitching at the toes and heels. "It's because I got frostbite once." He stopped to sip his hot chocolate, which he'd ordered topped with miniature marshmallows.

I continued unlacing my ski shoes.

"Ma left me, Tommy, and Cheryl in the car all night one time. It was the middle of winter and colder than a well digger's ass outside. We were in the backseat, huddled together, trying to keep warm. I gave my socks to Cheryl, poor kid, to keep her from freezing. But I got frostbite and now my feet have terrible circulation." Dad looked sadly down at his toes. His blue eyes sparkled like two swimming pools.

"It was nice of you to give your socks away like that."

"Yeah. But now my feet won't ever stay warm."

When, a few days later, Dad dropped me home in Watertown, I cried over his generous and broken heart until Mom told me to knock it off.

The decision of whether to run from the law was a purely senti-mental one. Dad had to assess the worth of his life, which he mea-sured by the level of devotion emanating from his friends and lovers and family. Prison meant slow, lonely death. Running, while des-perate and impossible, was at least doing something. Reaching. But reaching for what?

He weighed his options over drinks and dinner with people he'd known for decades. Most weren't aware of the dark problem festering behind his pulsing temples. My father could hide enormous secrets. The marshals, during their long hunt, would interview a man who said that just after Dad's arrest, the two met at a bar called Archie's in a Minneapolis suburb. The man's name is blacked out at the top of the police report, but he claimed to have known Dad since 1959. The friend became visibly upset when the police told him about my father's crime-riddled past. He said he'd had no idea. It wasn't the bank robberies or the counterfeiting that disturbed him so much as the fact that Dad hadn't trusted him. The reporting officer wrote that the man apparently "considered himself and the subject stronger 'friends' than the subject did."

My father phoned his longtime friend Jimmy. Around 1980, Jimmy had been one of the original sales agents in my father's real estate firm, RED Inc. Dad thought the name, which stood for Real Estate & Development Incorporated, extremely clever and he proudly distributed company pens that expelled red ink. Unfortunately, the acronym turned out to be apt.

Jimmy was impossibly thin, charming, and borderline crazy. He had secrets himself and therefore never plied my father with questions. Jimmy lived with his wife and two children in a resort town in northern Minnesota, where he also owned a lake cabin. On the phone, Dad told Jimmy he wanted to drive up to "clear his head." Jimmy knew something was wrong, though Dad came north quite often and even had his own fishing pole at Jimmy's cabin. When he visited, he usually brought armloads of gifts—sheets and towels, toys and videos for the kids—all purchased at Wal-Mart. He'd become so fond of the town where Jimmy lived, he considered moving there.

The police labeled my father a "master counterfeiter" and crowed about the nearly $20 million they'd seized (the money took three weeks to count, they bragged); the truth, however, was less glamorous. Dad had barely been scraping by at the print shop in Navarre, west of Minneapolis. His legitimate clients were few, and counterfeiting was methodical work, slow going. In fact, the bulk of what the cops discovered were practice bills, unfit to pass. My father wasn't rich. Nor, it seems, was he looking to get rich. He labored in the shop, next door to an auto supply store in a broken-down strip mall, trying to earn enough to purchase a house and decent car. He also hoped to buy a restaurant in the town where Jimmy lived. The restaurant, called the Harbor Inn, had languished on the real estate market for months. Jimmy negotiated with the owner and Dad passed his counterfeit in order to gather the $1,200 down payment. He was one day from mailing the payment when the police raided his shop. The money was in a padded yellow envelope on the desk.

Given my father's tendency to shade the truth, it's difficult to say who among his friends and relatives were aware of the counterfeiting. Certainly there were those who guessed he was doing something illegal. Cheryl, for instance. She lived with Dad in an apartment complex called the Bryantwood. She ran a mailing service next door to his shop, the two offices separated by a glass door. She had permission to fill out and sign his name to checks. Cheryl says she suspected payroll fraud, but when she inquired about it, Dad said, "You don't want to know." When she asked what he'd do if caught doing whatever he was doing, he said, "I'll just kill myself."

The facts became glaringly obvious to Cheryl the day the police charged in. Because she had signed for the Brownsville package, she was detained alongside Dad. The police ransacked the Bryantwood, ruining furniture and laying their hands on family heirlooms and other personal belongings. Cheryl was never charged, but she says the Secret Service followed her around and dropped in on friends solely for the sake of embarrassing her. She claims they attached a tracking device to her car. Records show the Marshals Service placed a "mail cover"—which allows the police access to information appearing on the outsides of envelopes and packages delivered to a home—on Cheryl's address. The marshals suspected that while on the lam, Dad might write his sister a letter. Cheryl had always seemed a little touchy, defensive; with the cops on her tail, she had reason.

On January 21, just two days before the hearing, Dad arrived in northern Minnesota and met Jimmy at the American Legion. Though they spoke for three or four hours, my father didn't go into detail about the arrest. He said only that he had "a little problem." Jimmy offered Dad a loan, but Dad refused it. "I guess I'm just a frustrated artist," he said as he stepped into his brown 1986 Oldsmobile Regency. Such a dull, practical car. Then he drove off, heading south through the snow and poplar trees.

Dad had always been a natural behind the wheel. He'd lean back in the seat and sling his right arm over the passenger headrest. He smoked when he drove, a pack of cigarettes jutting from the seat crack along with the Chap Stick and nasal spray he was constantly administering. (The mingling of these three elements created Dad's particular smell.) My father smoked Carlton 100s because he was forever trying to quit. Carltons have little holes around the filters so the smoker gets a lighter and ostensibly less harmful drag—Dad plugged the holes with his fingers. When it came time to light up, he removed both hands from the wheel and steered with his knees.

Not even halfway back to Minneapolis, my father took a room at the Brainerd Holiday Inn. Perhaps he stopped because he was tired, though that seems unlikely given the urgency of his situation. Probably he stopped because this breezy resort town was the best place to think. He could consider his future amid good memories, the best he had. Dad haunted. He'd go miles out of his way to pass places of significance in order to gather the faint echo of childhood or lost love. By staring at the artifact, he assured himself of what was true.

I imagine he did some haunting in Brainerd. Likely, he drove past the cabin on Round Lake he'd built so many years before. (He certainly would have been mortified to find that the new owners had painted it tan.) He probably stopped by the piece of land he purchased on Gull Lake after selling the Round Lake property. Maybe he remembered the time we slept there in the pop-up camper; he shook us awake in the middle of the night to watch a skunk with its head stuck inside a Peanut Buster Parfait cup. And when it started getting late, there was only one option for dinner: Dad's favorite supper club, Bar Harbor, with its crusty au gratin potatoes, stiff drinks, and an atmosphere that hadn't changed a stitch in thirty years.

Perhaps my father gleaned warmth from the scenery. Perhaps he plucked reassurance from the words uttered by familiar faces. Whatever the reason, by the time he checked out of the Holiday Inn the next morning, he'd decided to run. Get a little more freedom. Test love. Cross his fingers for a miracle.

He drove the rest of the way to Minneapolis. He parked the Olds in the lot behind the Bryantwood and dashed upstairs to his and Cheryl's third-floor apartment. She wasn't home. He gathered belongings into a brown vinyl suitcase: shirts, pants, underwear, toilet articles, mementos. He packed two handguns and ammunition.

Then he met Cheryl at a bar to say good-bye. The two sat in the back, smoking in silence because the police might be listening in. She was visibly angry and worried. Dad muttered, "Please don't hate me, but I have to go. I'd shoot myself in the head right now if it'd help." Cheryl answered that it wouldn't. She asked how he'd survive. Dad scribbled on a piece of paper and slid it to her. The note said: *The cops missed almost $30,000 in counterfeit I had hidden in the car.*

The next day at 11 A.M., the judge, attorneys, and bailiffs gathered in a Minneapolis courtroom for Dad's hearing. When he didn't show, they issued a warrant for his arrest. He was officially charged with five counts of counterfeiting and one count of failing to appear. The police said that added up to a possible $1.25 million fine and seventy-three years in prison. Reading that in the papers probably didn't give my father much incentive to come back.

A few days later, a handwritten letter arrived at the office of the Secret Service. It was postmarked Illinois and dated the day of the hearing.

January 23, 1995

[blank], Agent
U.S. Secret Service
U.S. Courthouse
110 So. 4th St.
Mpls, MN 55401

Dear Jim,

Sorry for the disappearing act but I sensed an urgency on your part and felt that you were preparing something, something to increase the charges so that my bond would be revoked at the preliminary this morning. I'm not quite ready to face the music, but I will be soon. Also, I said I would cooperate *completely* with you after talking to an attorney, but you ignored that, apparently believing I'd lied, and harassed and hassled a lot of innocent people. NO ONE ELSE IS INVOLVED. No one in my address book is involved. None of my friends knows anything. There is no more bogus money— you have it all (with the exception of a few notes overlooked in my trunk which I'll try not to pass unless I run out of money. Sorry.).

As soon as you and your people give up the notion of a gigantic international conspiracy and stop intimidating and accusing everybody I'm acquainted with, I'll give myself up.

Regards,
John Vogel

Vogel means bird in German

7

DAD HAD FALSE TEETH. But I wouldn't know that until I was seventeen and happened across a tube of denture cream hidden at the bottom of a drawer. My whole life I'd been watching him chew, and never once did he mention slippage or the rough-edged cookie crumbs that certainly lodged under his plastic gums. He was vigilant about his image. Dad was vain just like Carly Simon said, but also he was concerned about being judged. He stood outside himself and picked, his worry bordering on paranoia. He issued directives that made no rational sense: *Don't tell Tom I said that. Don't tell Debbie I was here. Your mother doesn't need to know about this. If Bob asks, that wasn't me at the grocery store.*

It was out of character, then, when, just after my twelfth birthday, on the way home from the Brainerd cabin, Dad cut over to Highway 71 leading to Sauk Centre, the town of his birth. He suggested the two of us take a tour. This forthright and comparatively unguarded act approached optimistic.

Sauk Centre lies about a hundred miles northwest of Minneapolis. It was founded in the mid-1800s by a small, determined group of Canadians, Germans, and uptight Anglo Protestants from the New England states. The townspeople were predominantly wheat farmers and mill workers. Later, Sauk Centre would be dubbed the "butter capital of Minnesota." The town's streets are lined with quaint old brick and wood houses and stores, not unlike those depicted in Norman Rockwell's wishful paintings. Rockwell was one of my father's all-time-favorite artists.

"Sinclair Lewis was born here, you know." Dad pointed to a sign indicating this fact. "In the nineteen twenties, he wrote a book called *Main Street* based on Sauk Centre."

I had only a vague notion of who Lewis was. "Have you read the book?"

"The town was all up in arms about it." Dad was never much for books.

We weaved up one street and down the next, my father gesturing toward various landmarks, both Lewis-related and personal. We slowed way down when we got to Sinclair Lewis Park.

"My aunt Florence used to play piano in the gazebo here. Classical piano." He emphasized the word *classical* to show the woman possessed taste. "Florence had the longest fingers anyone had ever seen. They stretched halfway across the piano keyboard. You have small hands. That's going to be difficult for you, honey."

I stretched my fingers out as far as possible and confirmed that, indeed, my hands were insufficient. Despite the lessons with Sister Mary Margaret, I'd never become an accomplished pianist.

"You have fine features. You get them from me. See, look at my nose. You have my nose, and my eyes. Your ears are tiny." He grabbed at my ear, then pretended to capture my nose and show it to me. "People are going to have to look closely to see what's beautiful about you."

I liked the idea.

"As I've always said, you're a swan among geese, honey, a rose among wildflowers. You're special. Someday you'll realize that. . . . Of course, there's your mother's side of the family too. They're as huge as water buffalo. You're going to have to watch your weight."

Silence.

"Seriously, Florence's fingers were this long!" Dad held his left hand about four inches beyond the fingertips of his right. He gazed wistfully out the window. "When she played, the whole town came to listen."

He was genuinely proud of Florence, the only relative he bragged about. Florence was Dad's aunt on his father's side. Though he didn't know much about the Vogels, he was utterly fascinated by them. He described the family in regal terms and legitimized their skybound status by informing me, over and over, that "Vogel means 'bird' in German." He thought the translation fitting and poetic. And, really, it was. Dad's father had flown the coop early on, leaving Grandma Margaret to raise Dad, Cheryl, and Tom on her own.

Grandma was herself a puzzle. She donned the proper uniform: apron, polyester pants, and white gardening sneakers. She served neatly sliced tuna sandwiches on white bread. At the same time, she dyed her hair red and wore bright lipstick that bled into the wrinkles around her mouth. She sucked in when she whistled, lending otherwise cheerful tunes a distracted, faintly sinister quality. I dreaded visiting her house, but Dad dragged me and my brother and sister there whenever we came to Minneapolis, as if it were a duty or a payment. She and my father sparred silently, she at the sink washing dishes and he with his long legs crossed at the kitchen table.

Grandma described her parents, Mary and Patrick, as shanty Irish, a term used in America around the turn of the twentieth century to describe Irish folk who were poor and seemingly low-down, especially those who lived in shacks made of old lumber and sheet iron. The lace-curtain Irish were as penniless as the shanty Irish, but they harbored big ideas: they'd put up fancy curtains for appearances, even in a hovel.

"The only difference between lace-curtain Irish and shanty Irish," Grandma quipped, leveling her wolflike eyes, "is that the lace-curtain Irish will take the dishes out of the sink before pissing in it."

Mary and Patrick were farmers outside Sauk Centre. They were devout Catholics and piss poor, which set them at odds with most of the townspeople. To quote a good resident of *Main Street*: "People who make more than ten thousand a year or less than eight hundred are wicked." Grandma Margaret said if she or any of her five siblings crossed into a yard on the way home from school, they drew peeks from behind curtains and curses from doorways: "Git on your way, you Cat-lics!" (her imitation of the German accent). Mary and Patrick didn't bear the burden well. They were stern, even violent. Patrick supposedly beat Grandma's brother Elmer, who struck out for Detroit at age thirteen. Elmer swept floors at an auto factory, worked his way up to management, and earned a cool fortune selling black-market tires during World War II. The rest of the family stuck it out near Sauk Centre and managed to forge a decent reputation for themselves. Another of Margaret's brothers, Warren, won an election, becoming a two-term sheriff in neighboring Todd County.

Dad gestured toward Sauk Centre city hall. "My uncle Warren worked there. I lived with him for a while."

I'd seen pictures of Warren. He had a big, red face, pocked like a grapefruit. I said it didn't sound pleasant, living with a man who bore a mug like that.

Dad fingered his cigarette. "It wasn't too bad."

Grandma Margaret suffered polio as a girl; she limped. But she was pretty. Slender and small, with bright eyes and thick red hair, she grew to look a little like Kate Hepburn. She was smart and spirited and adept at getting what she wanted. As a young woman, what she wanted was Joseph Vogel.

Joe must have stood out in tiny Sauk Centre—topping six feet, classically handsome, a soldier in the army, and from a good family besides. His parents, Agnes and Benedict, were property owners and looked down on Mary and Patrick and Margaret (later, when Cheryl would visit her grandma Vogel, she wouldn't be allowed to sit all the way back in the chairs for fear of grease spots). Joe was wild, a black sheep who drank and gambled. He and Margaret married in the middle of World War II and set up house in Sauk Cen-

tre. They had their first child on October 4, 1942. Dad's birth cer-
tificate lists him as John Bryson Vogel, but Grandma often spelled
his name Jon, as though it didn't matter one way or the other. Dad
was a handsome baby, with dark hair and shimmering eyes—he
looked exactly like Joe.

The union didn't last long. Joe, a chronic philanderer, ran off for
good with a skater from the traveling Ice Capades. Decades later,
when Joe was dying of throat cancer, he found himself destitute and
alone, a stranger to his children. He'd failed to attend his mother's
funeral, and he'd been exorcised from his father's will. When the
gravediggers went to make a hole for Joe at Sauk Centre's cemetery,
one of his brothers stood before the backhoe and tried to stop it
from being dug.

Margaret found herself alone with three kids and no money at a
time when society was dead set against that sort of thing. She
moved the family to Minneapolis and took a job as an accountant
at a Jewish temple, despite her anti-Semitism. (She and Joe had this
in common: on the back of a photo of Joe looking to the horizon
like a proud aviator, he wrote, *Isn't this awful—I look Jewish don't I.*)
The temple paid cash, allowing Grandma to sign up for welfare.
Once, after a few glasses of wine, she admitted using aliases to gar-
ner multiple checks: "If they caught me, I'd never again see the light
of day!"

Still a young woman, Grandma liked bars and she liked men.
She deposited the children with her brothers or mother. When Dad
was a small boy, she moved him to Mary's house and visited only
when she knew her son wouldn't be there. Her skewed reasoning
dictated that if he saw her, he'd only miss her more. One day, Dad
was playing in the backyard when he spied her taillights turning out
of the driveway. He ran to the road, yelling and waving his arms, but
Margaret kept driving. Dad pursued her. He was found a couple of
hours later by the side of the road, passed out from heat stroke. It's
a story Margaret later told with pride, as it proved his devotion to
her. "Tied to his mother's apron strings," she said, shaking her head.

We pulled up Main Street, past the Ben Franklin and the Main Street Theatre, and turned onto Sinclair Lewis Avenue. Dad pointed out Lewis's boyhood home, which had recently been restored. We passed a church school.

"I went here before we moved to Minneapolis and I started at the basilica. I was an altar boy. The priests were so mean, they'd ask you a question and if you didn't answer loud enough, they'd yell, 'Louder, boy!' Can you imagine? This booming, 'Louder, boy!'? It scared the hell out of you."

"Do you still believe in God?"

"I think hell is right here on earth."

The tour ended with a glimpse of what Dad said was the Vogel family home. He drove past in silence, as if it were a shrine, his eyes welling up. I couldn't figure it out. He'd received so little from these people, yet he obviously considered them superior to his mother's family and even himself. My father harbored frightening ideas about race and worthiness, which I assume derived from a sense of personal shame. The Vogels—the Germans—came from better stock. They'd made that clear. And, as the rejected often do, Dad tried like hell to transmogrify a mere genetic link into a substantial and portentous one.

He lit a cigarette. "I'd like to visit Europe. Maybe rent a car and travel leisurely through it, look up our relatives in Germany, probably near the Schwarzwald. I'll take you along."

"Where?"

"The Black Forest. It's where our family comes from. You know, any Vogel can go there and be welcomed with open arms. We own part of the Vogel mountains. In Germany, we're practically royalty."

He looked over at me. "Always remember, blood is thicker than water."

8

Late February 1995

DAD HADN'T SOUGHT refuge at my apartment like the marshals thought he would. Nor had he called. I, for one, didn't expect him to knock on my door; that would have been too vulnerable an act. But, just the same, I was convinced I'd see him again. It didn't seem possible that a figure as significant as a father—my father—could simply vanish. Besides, I was arrogant and still considered myself the apple of his eye. I was sure he'd find a way to see me, even if it meant bumping into me on the sidewalk.

He was nowhere and everywhere—among crowds, reflected off store windows. I spotted him almost daily. But then the tall man with the slouching shoulders and graying hair would turn to face me in the produce section or draw nearer at the bus stop and reveal himself a stranger. I began to notice how much Dad resembled Johnny Carson and Harrison Ford and Tommy Smothers and Jason Robards, Jr., and Paul Newman. I've heard this phenomenon often accompanies a death. And it almost felt like my father was dead, except that when someone's dead you know how his story ends. The dead are beyond decision or deed.

When I returned home from work each night, I checked the bushes outside my building to make sure he wasn't lurking in the shadows. If there was a hang-up click on my answering machine, I imagined it had been him.

One evening, my machine played back a sigh. I was standing over it, still wearing a jacket and book bag. The sigh was heavy, definitely male. It was Dad. I was sure of it. I pictured him standing at a pay phone in a parking lot, peering furtively toward the street, clutching a Styrofoam cup of coffee. I saw him frustrated, slamming the receiver down.

He'll call back, I thought. Maybe he'll call back.

My friends were mostly oblivious to this drama of expectation. Rarely did I discuss Dad or his penchant for crime. I was embarrassed at first. Later, I pretended he didn't exist. With meticulously honed outrage, I pondered his ill deeds, assuring myself that I was good, my mother's daughter, nothing like Dad at all. What I knew was that I was split—part good and part bad, with the good winning out. So far.

I once thought my destiny included knocking off a convenience store. There wasn't any question about it: I'd simply up and commit robbery one day. I had broken laws—stealing, setting fires, selling drugs—and I'd justified these acts by a personalized system of right and wrong, an internal logic. That's how you battle wickedness; you develop internal logic. *This is okay to do. That is not.* It was Mom's genes, derived from Abe Lincoln's, that kept me from going all the way. Violence was out of bounds and so was lying. Deception was more damning than stealing. It corrupted one's relationship to reality. Dad had deceived Mom and that had been the worst part.

I credited impulses to lie—fleeting, lingering, or irresistible—to "little Dad moments." To keep the little Dad moments in check, I kept my father's hold on me in check by putting as much distance between us as possible. When I did share details of the counterfeiting bust with friends, I described the quality of the bills and the enormity of the hunt. I did so with bravado, as if describing a celebrity who'd once baby-sat me.

I joked that the marshals were following me and secretly hoped they were. A police tail would have branded me still-important-to-Dad and set me against the law, where I was usually most comfortable. Gizzard, one of my best friends, took to waving at helicopters from the highway in my Escort. She strode into my *City Pages* cubicle one afternoon and leaned over my shoulder, flutter-waving out the window toward the parking garage across the street. "Just in case they're watching," she said with a wink and a grin. Side by side, we leaned into the window and hammed enthusiastically. I peered at the garage, examining the shadows.

There was no real information, just imagination and muted hysteria. I tracked the daily newspapers for updates on the case, but found not a single word of lead, arrest, or location. Nobody seemed to know where he was or where he might be headed. This was especially disconcerting to Mom, who worried he might show up at the farm where she lived with her husband. She knew Dad possessed guns, as he always had. Cheryl, it turned out later, had talked with him by phone. When she told him a friend of hers was going down south for vacation, Dad responded that he was "going down south too. Way south." Cheryl must have been too busy fending off counterfeiting charges to relay to the rest of the family anything he'd said.

The marshals were my only resource, and they weren't much help. I knew why. During a conversation with Mom, they'd expressed their belief that I wouldn't turn Dad over if he came to me for help. Knowing that they knew this lent our curbside chats an air of espionage. They were suspicious of me, yet they acted completely at ease. They inquired as to how I was holding up and revealed bits of what their investigation had uncovered, but only the select details they wanted verified or embellished upon in order to determine where Dad might be hiding.

"How goes the search?" I was in the backseat again.

"We haven't found John yet. But you know that. We're interviewing his associates. We've got some leads."

"I'd be curious to know who you've talked to."

"Oh, a lot of people. The other day we interviewed one of John's oldest friends. They were in prison together in 1960."

I was surprised they'd used the term *prison*. I knew Dad had been incarcerated before he and Mom met, but I'd been told he was sent to a juvenile detention center. The distinction was important to me: the difference between a troubled teenager and a congenital thief. Dad was certainly the former. He'd bombed out at Catholic school, earning As one term and Ds the next (though he always got high marks for neatness and in art). His report cards show that he had trouble with authority and with "respect and courtesy" as they pertained to "rules and regulations." When he was fifteen, he was sent briefly to a boys' home for stealing a car. At sixteen, he moved on to knocking over convenience stores. He'd wait until the clerk was distracted and slip into a back room or under a display table. Thin and lithe, he went unnoticed. After the store closed, he'd empty the cash register and leave. He was seventeen when the cops showed up at the house to arrest him.

To lend the robberies a noble air, Dad claimed to have given the proceeds to Grandma Margaret to help with household bills. He even said she'd encouraged the holdups. Then he lobbed his signature heartbreaking twist: it had been his mother who had turned him in. Grandma put her own spin on the tale, explaining that she'd called the police because Dad had graduated to armed holdups using a sawed-off shotgun. She said she'd been worried sick he'd get hurt.

"Prison? Don't you mean juvenile detention?"

The agents glanced at one another. "No, it was prison. John was convicted of second-degree robbery. He was sentenced as an adult in January 1960 and sent to the state prison in St. Cloud. He was paroled about two years later."

It hit me that St. Cloud was the prison Dad had repeatedly driven us past on the way to Brainerd. I felt untethered. Not just because my perception of the prison—of those drives—had been wrong for twenty years, but because Dad had so competently hidden the truth. He'd answered my childish questions without hesitation. I wondered why he'd chosen that particular highway. After all, there were other routes to Brainerd. Maybe seeing the monolithic gray wall served as a sort of deterrent to criminal behavior. Or maybe he'd convinced himself that his stint at St. Cloud never happened. Maybe deep down, even unconsciously, he divined his ultimate fate and couldn't help but look straight at it.

"You didn't know?"

I snapped to the present. My face felt hot. "I knew something about it."

"He fooled a lot of people."

"I guess." I didn't like being called a sucker, no matter how sympathetically it was packaged. And I didn't like the agents pretending to know Dad.

"We understand John spent a bit of time in Florida. You and your brother and sister traveled there with him, right?" The agents didn't mention the impetus for this particular line of questioning, but Dad's fake bills were surfacing all over the country. Several had turned up in Florida.

In 1978, Dad flew the three of us to St. Petersburg as a big surprise. We'd looked forward to the trip for months without knowing what it was we were looking forward to. Dad refused to unveil the details until just before heading to the airport. "We're going to Florida! The plane leaves in four hours!" We were ecstatic. We'd never been so far from home, never once seen the ocean.

Dad stood at the ticket counter and peeled hundred-dollar bills from a roll he kept in his right front pocket. He always paid cash for everything. We boarded the jet. If Dad was nervous about flying— he harbored a lifelong fear of heights—he didn't show it, even during takeoff. He ordered a couple of gimlets and flirted with the stewardesses. Before we knew it, a nice-looking brunette was pinning us all with plastic captain's wings.

In Florida, Dad's friend Stuart met us at the gate. He was an oafish man with shaggy brown hair and a thick mustache. He looked like Rob Reiner circa *All in the Family*. On the way to the baggage claim, Nick and I trotted behind Stuart and Dad snickering

Meathead jokes. We piled into Meathead's car and sped down the highway, passing white beaches that looked as though something had been erased. The land was flat and wide. Spiky, glossy plants sprung from the ground, supported by beefy stems tangled like snakes. The air felt warm and plump against my lips. It smelled fruity and salty and was imbued with everlasting heat. This was the perfect place to nurture an ambitious dream.

Stuart dropped us at a small furnished apartment, decorated in browns and lime green. Everything we needed was provided, even dishes and silverware. It was a winter rental, available cheap because it was July and nearing 110 degrees.

We spent most of the next week at the beach, a short walk from the apartment. Sometimes on the way there, we got waylaid while Liz pursued the tiny green lizards that dotted the trees and sidewalks. The water was warm and welcoming, the waves like hands clapping. We rode the swells, coming up after each lunge with swimsuit-loads of wet sand. One afternoon, Liz came up with more than that. She stood in the shallow water screaming, her arms high in the air. Dad jumped up from his beach towel and dashed into the Gulf. Suctioned halfway up her calf was a small, reddish starfish. Dad peeled it off, then showed it to Liz and asked whether she wanted to keep it as a souvenir. She cheered up a bit. Back at the apartment, my father laid the starfish on a slab of cement to dry. We watched it slowly die in the sun. When the starfish began to curl in on itself, Dad set a flowerpot on top of it.

My father owned a boat, a forty-one-foot Owens Cutter sloop built in the 1940s by the Hinckley company of Maine. Dad said Hinckley crafted the most elegant sailboats in the world. His was a classic: all mahogany, quick, with long, clean lines. The Cadillac of sailboats, as he called it, was dry-docked at a marina near Clearwater, where Dad was finishing up a long and rather remarkable restoration.

We viewed it for the first time soon after our arrival. We'd spent the morning with Debbie nursing painful, tomato-red sunburns.

She'd cracked open a couple of aloe leaves and rubbed the gooey innards on our backs, a level of holistic medicine unfamiliar to me. We arrived at the marina coated in sunscreen and wearing over-sized, cover-all T-shirts. The boat looked huge and awkward out of the water, mounted as it was on a makeshift wooden frame. When Debbie called from the ground, Dad appeared on deck, smiling. He wore a grimy white shirt, jeans, and a beat-up straw hat. His whiskers were becoming a beard.

He climbed jauntily down the orange ladder propped against the side of the boat, a cigarette pressed between his lips. Intent on wow-ing us, he pulled from his back pocket a small stack of photographs documenting the months of slow progress. The boat had come down from Michigan in rough shape, nicked and peeling and dried out. There was a gash in its side where the transporting company had run it into a bridge. The belowdeck cabin—the sleeping quar-ters, the galley, the head—had arrived a shambles too. One of the photos showed Dad cutting a curved piece of wood with a jigsaw. In another, he was sanding a metal fitting held in his lap. A third depicted Dad taking a break in the galley. He looked exhausted, eyes puffy, knees at his chest. A small carton of milk stood on the counter next to him, along with a bean-bag-bottomed ashtray overflowing with butts. Tools were strewn everywhere.

Ever since my father was a teenager, he'd fantasized about sailing around the world. In what I now know was St. Cloud prison, he ordered subscriptions to sailing magazines. He lingered over images of sailors living exotic lives of leisure, visiting faraway places with-out worry of jobs or even shirts. This was a community of sophisti-cated, fun-loving slackers; Dad desperately wanted to join up. He lusted after freedom, the sort of freedom most free people never experience.

Formerly, the boat had been painted dull black with a red stripe; now it was gleaming white with a classy gold stripe. The oiled decks showed off the beauty of the mahogany. The bronze fittings shim-mered. Dad had purchased a new sail and jib, which were rolled under a peppy, yellow-and-white-striped cover. Belowdeck, the living space was cozy. The galley was in full working order. The bench seats and beds were fitted with new pads and covers. He'd chosen a name and painted it across the back in gold: "Razzmatazz."

Our visit to Florida, it turned out, was timed so we could accompany Dad on the maiden voyage of the *Razzmatazz*. The boat was moved to a slip from dry dock with a huge crane. Not long after, we were motoring into the harbor, with Dad bragging that the boat's powerful engine could dislodge us from any sandbar. Its sixty-foot mast was too tall to fit under the bridge that separated us from the Gulf. Dad explained that we had to honk in order to alert the bridge keeper to open the bridge. "The guy sleeps in that booth," he told me, pointing. "We've got to wake him up." He handed me a can with a red plastic cone at the top and told me to count to three before pushing the button two times in a row. Then he dashed off, giggling with his fingers in his ears. I pushed the button as directed, releasing a deafening blast. It sounded like an air raid siren. I blew it once more. When the bridge started to open, I swelled with pride.

We made it only a short distance up the coast before getting stuck on a sandbar. Dad revved the motor until gray billows filled the air, but the boat didn't budge. Frustrated and embarrassed, he loaded the anchor into the small dinghy and rowed out a ways. He dropped the anchor into the water and used it to winch us free. The voyage was over, my father's enthusiasm extinguished. He sold the *Razzmatazz* soon after, claiming that it leaked.

Back in Watertown, Mom was unaware we'd gone to Florida. When she called Grandma Margaret's house asking after us, Margaret claimed we were at the zoo or playing in the yard. She reassured Mom we were having a wonderful time and offered to pass on a hello. Then one afternoon when Dad wasn't around, my brother made an unauthorized phone call from the apartment. Nick told Mom about the seagulls and all the colorful harbors we'd seen. She interrupted to ask where in God's name Nick was and Nick told her.

Mom phoned Margaret and threatened to report Dad to the

authorities for violating their court-ordered custody agreement. The next day we were on a plane home.

"Your mother said John took you there without her knowledge."

"That's right. She got really pissed when she found out."

"You're smiling."

"It was a fun trip." I said nothing more. I didn't want the marshals tainting this memory with fact or innuendo. I didn't want them suggesting that Dad had planned to abscond with us to Tahiti or use the boat to transport drugs.

"Do you think John would go back to Florida?"

"I really don't know."

"Did he ever talk with you about Mexico?"

"No, never. Mexico is way too broken-down for Dad. Why?"

"Just wondering."

That night, I lay awake in bed recalling, word for word, my conversation with the marshals. I looked for cracks, tried to decipher whether they'd unintentionally revealed something of importance. The Mexico question was intriguing, though I was convinced Dad would stick closer to home.

9

We left Watertown and everything we knew

DATING WAS DIFFICULT for Mom. Romance is complicated for any single mother. First you have to find a man who doesn't mind kids, then he has to be a man your kids won't despise. Whenever Mom introduced us to suitors she liked, we acted like jerks. We interpreted every attempt to befriend us as ass kissing, and we always found something wrong, a fatal flaw: Ferris gobbled Certs and was too skinny. Guy was boring and wore brown corduroy suits that made noise when he walked. Then Mom met Doc. We liked him immediately.

Doc was a heavyset, dark-skinned Norwegian with wavy black hair. He was sturdy and smart and he had a hearty laugh. Most evenings, he'd pull up to our house in his orange Jeep, loaded with groceries. He brought delicacies like glazed donuts and steaks. Doc was a veterinarian and one of the wealthiest men in town.

When Grandma Bernice visited, Doc handed her a fork and carving knife and placed her at the head of the table. That was his way of imposing formality on my rag-and-bone family. He led prayers before dinner; he encouraged us to serve side dishes from bowls, rather than pans; and he attempted to enlighten us with the finer things, reciting poems—usually Edgar Allan Poe's "The

Raven" or "Lenore"—which we were supposed to memorize. He even made a painting, a copy of a print that hung on Mom's bedroom wall. The picture was of men maneuvering a small fishing boat through stormy waters. Doc presented his painting to Mom in the middle of the night. He'd signed it in code: *To a friend, from a friend.*

Doc was married.

Once, when his wife and children were out of town, he invited us to his house. Wide-eyed and careful like hicks at a museum, we entered the spacious home with its multiple bathrooms and plush carpeting. We watched TV and ate fried chicken at the dining room table. Family portraits glared at us. Doc monitored my mother, eagerly awaiting her comments of appreciation and awe. He was wildly in love with her, and he was also probably in love with the way we all looked at him. He was like some big, dark Santa offering a glimpse of a better life. Seeing if it fit.

I was instructed to sleep in his son John's room, which was in the basement. John was my age, the star of the football team at school. I marveled at the size of his room, his clothing and stereo, all he had that I didn't. Then I felt sorry for him because his dad was cheating on his mom. I opted not to sleep in his bed. Instead, I sat in a chair all night with headphones on, listening to REO Speedwagon's *Hi Infidelity.*

Doc tried to ease out of his marriage gracefully, but it's nearly impossible to make graceful exits in small towns. People talked mean, cruel talk—especially at church, the fulcrum of our community and domain of the town's women. (The disapproval was inter-denominational, since we were Congregational and Doc's family was Lutheran.) There was only one way for Mom and Doc to be together, for us to be able to walk down the street as a real family. We would have to leave town.

It was toward the end of ninth grade, when I was fifteen, that Mom broke the news. Doc had been kicked by a bull a few years prior, seriously injuring his back. A surgeon had welded two of his vertebrae together, but it hadn't helped. Mom said Doc was giving up veterinary medicine. He'd landed a new job as an inspector in a meatpacking plant in Cedar Rapids, Iowa.

I was nearly hysterical. "What am I supposed to do in Iowa? Everybody here knows me!" It was bizarre, this sudden fondness toward my classmates, my standing. "I'll be just another face in the crowd!"

At that, I'd crossed a line. A common put-down in my family was "Who do you think you are?" Egocentrism was fodder for mockery. Mine were not serious concerns. Nick broke into a laugh.

Considering the number of times I'd threatened to pack off to California, it was difficult to convince anyone at school I was really moving. However, when I didn't waver from the story, when word circulated that John's father was leaving with us, my classmates accepted that it was true. True, but inconsequential.

The prospect of leaving loosened something within me, some part I'd been holding steady and protecting—honor, hope for advancement. I'd been the good girl for so long, believing that just maybe I was the swan among geese like Dad said. I saw myself now outside the context of the town and its people. The old Jennifer could be ash-canned—a newer, pinker Jennifer emerging without the branding of the past. I could do anything I pleased before leaving, at no cost whatever to my reputation. My actions would be tested only against my personal desires and beliefs. Moving seemed a kind of suicide.

Mom felt guilty about uprooting us, which worked to my advantage. She let me stay out all night with the Chevette. How could she possibly enforce a curfew when I was being forced to leave my dear, dear friends and everything I'd known? And besides, Mom was wrestling her own worries. She had to find a buyer for the house, pack all our belongings, and keep peace with our new lord and master, Doc.

Doc's character had transformed since we'd agreed to go away with him. He'd soured. He drank more heavily than usual, polishing off gallon jugs of Black Velvet and peppermint schnapps, which he mixed together and guzzled without ice. For the first time, he used words like *spoiled* and *brat*. He demanded rather than asked. He altogether stopped wearing shirts in the evening, so his hairy belly swung unfettered. But Mom had made too many promises to pull out of the deal. All she could do was muster that old pioneer spirit. And pop the top off a bottle of vodka.

I'd threatened to move in with Dad many times over the years. It was a ploy, usually lobbed during an argument with Mom. I never really wanted to change sides, to stake out a new life in a strange city. I only knew that Mom would soften at the thought of it. I don't remember the particular circumstances that led me to make the threat that afternoon, in the living room amid all those half-filled moving boxes. I don't recall if I'd had a fight with Doc, if I'd weighed my options and genuinely opted for Minneapolis. Maybe, as usual, I merely wanted something.

I said it with force. "I'll just go live with Dad!"

Mom became irritated and answered, as she always did, that Dad only offered to take me because he knew I wouldn't accept. "You kids are like his hunting dogs. He only runs you when he feels like it." He wouldn't know the first thing about raising a daughter, she said. He wasn't built for fatherhood. "Do you think he's going to put food on the table and buy you clothes and get you to the doctor when you need to go?" She was pointing now with her index finger.

I interrupted. "Living with Dad has got to be better than living with you!"

Mom looked stricken. Then she spouted the roadblock phrase that had sent my imagination reeling since I was a small child. "There are things about your father you don't know," she said.

There was plenty about my father I did know, thanks to various slips and outbursts over the years. I knew that he didn't pay child support, that he lived well at our expense. I knew he lied about things and was crazy enough to occasionally believe those lies. I knew he was crooked in his business dealings. I knew he'd burned down at least three buildings for profit, mostly to collect insurance settlements. And I knew he'd made life hell for Mom. Out on the Annandale farm, when she'd sat at the kitchen table staring at the blue Plymouth, she'd been plotting, obsessively turning a plan. She would tell us we were going to Grandma Bernice's house, start the engine, and lock us inside the garage.

I couldn't imagine that this lurking information, these things I didn't know, could be more shocking than everything I was already aware of. So I asked the question I always asked: "Like what?"

"Wait until you're older."

"I am older!"

Perhaps it was the corrosive combination of stress and sadness surrounding the move, or maybe Mom was tired of being the heavy—she took us to the dentist, Dad took us to Disney World; she made us hamburger noodle hotdish, Dad served us medium-rare steaks and lobster tails. Maybe she really believed I'd go. In any case, Mom finally spilled the worst.

"Your dad can be violent." She paused, then sat down on the rust-colored living room chair next to a leopard-print pillow. Her cutoff shorts revealed varicose veins.

I paged back, searching for indications of violence in my father's gestures. He'd never raised a hand against me, Nick, or Liz. And, as far as I knew, he'd never touched Debbie. But he did have a quick temper. Once he'd raged at me for neglecting to put barbecue sauce on a slab of ribs he was grilling. Another time he exploded when I wouldn't drink Alka-Seltzer. "Just swallow it!" he'd demanded. "It won't kill you! Jesus Christ!" He'd gritted his teeth and growled furiously. It was the same snarl he hurled at traffic jams and "damned dirty flies." I remembered thinking he was mad about something else, something more important. The tantrum was like a lavatic bubble bursting through flat ground.

In a calm, steady tone, Mom told me about the apartment she'd shared with Dad early in their marriage. The bathroom door didn't close properly, and sometimes she felt as though somebody was watching her bathe. So she stabbed a knife into the doorjamb to lock it. A plywood wall ran alongside the tub, behind which was a closet. Dad told Mom he could build a shelf along the wall, upon which he could set a radio that was plugged in but with the volume turned down. Then, when she was steeped in suds, he could bang on the wall from the closet. The radio would fall into the tub and electrocute her. With a knife in the door, it would look like an accident. Mom stared at Dad's eyes, unable to discern whether he was serious because he was smiling.

Then came an apparent attempt on her life. We were leaving for Grandma Bernice's house. Dad put me in the car with him and asked Mom to drive separately with Nick, who was just an infant at the time. (Particularly irksome, Mom pointed out, was the fact that Dad's car was air conditioned, while hers was not.) Dad made Mom swear to follow him closely, to stay right on his bumper. On a two-lane highway, my father pulled into the left lane to pass a semi. Mom pulled out too. Dad dodged quickly back into traffic, leaving Mom to face an oncoming car. "The semi driver laid on his horn," Mom recalled. "The car coming toward me veered onto the shoulder and I threaded right down the middle. John pulled over and acted like he couldn't believe what had happened. But that was no accident. Your dad always had insurance on me. He probably had it on you kids too."

The story didn't rattle me the way it should have, maybe because I was in the car with my father, the car with the air-conditioning, the car that didn't almost get crushed by oncoming traffic.

Staring off at the large print of the handsome matador hanging on the far wall, Mom said that twice, their apartment almost caught fire. Once, she even discovered a mattress smoldering against the back door early on a Sunday morning when Dad wasn't home. The apartment was filled with smoke. Thankfully, a neighbor called the fire department.

Possibly these were just coincidences or misunderstandings, I thought. But then she told me about Elmer, Grandma Margaret's brother, the one who got rich selling black-market tires during the war. Occasionally, when I was a child, our family visited Elmer at his well-appointed home—an estate, really—near Paynesville, Minnesota. He was an unpleasant man. I remember getting into trouble once for picking a pear from one of his many perfect fruit trees. I toddled into the house, quite pleased, only to have Margaret snatch the pear away and shove it down the garbage disposal.

Around the time of these visits, Dad discovered he'd been named a benefactor in Elmer's will, information that made him restless. He couldn't get his mind off the money and what he would spend it on. From dark, mechanical obsession arose a plan. One day, Dad parked his car along a side street in a small town an hour outside Paynesville. He somehow got to the road Elmer drove along each day to retrieve his mail. Elmer spotted Dad standing there and picked him up. Acting upset, Dad said he'd been showing some clients a property—beautiful land, fantastic investment—and they'd left him stranded. He wondered if Elmer wanted to see the property. The two drove to a deserted farm a ways off the main road. When they got out of the car, Dad came up behind Elmer with a rock and struck him on the head. By some tremendous bit of luck, a lost trucker pulled up just then. Dad made like Elmer was drunk. He said he'd been trying to get the surly old man into the front seat.

That night, my father came home distraught. It looked as though Elmer would press charges. Dad gnawed his fingernails and wept on Mom's lap. He often confided in her, listing his insecurities, diagramming exactly how the deck had been stacked against him from the get-go. She'd listen and comfort, always sympathetic to wounded creatures. Then, by the light of day, Dad would regret his weakness and turn violent. He'd punch and kick her until she curled up into a ball.

Dad didn't tell Mom the truth about Elmer. He claimed, as he had to the trucker, that Elmer had been drunk and feisty. Mom, for her part, found the story unlikely, knowing that real estate agents always drive their own cars in order to maintain control. However, she didn't poke holes. She said that if Dad truly had nothing to hide, he should turn himself in to the police, which he did. He was promptly arrested and blamed Mom for it. Elmer eventually dropped the charges at Margaret's frantic urging, but not one of us was allowed near his home ever again.

Murder. There was nothing charming or James Bond about cold, vicious murder. "Do you think Dad really would have killed Elmer?"

"I don't know," Mom said. "I suppose. He used to brag to me that when he was a teenager and worked at Sears in Minneapolis, he beat a black man to death with a metal pipe. He said he snuck up behind him after the store closed. I don't know whether it was true."

That bit of information bothered me even more than the story about Elmer because the motivation was so much more terrifying. Years later, I would scour newspaper records, looking for mention of a beating behind the Sears building. When your father is an established villain, you tend to view things in gradations. It was important to me that he hadn't killed anyone, that he hadn't crossed into the territory of beasts. I found no mention of it in the papers. But it wouldn't have been unusual in the late 1950s or early '60s for the death of a black man to go unreported.

I grappled with renunciation and hope, the same, apparently, as Mom had done. By way of explanation or mitigation for my father's behavior, she said, "He wasn't all bad. Half the time, I felt sorry for him." When Dad was a boy, she said, he had a black dog that accompanied him on his newspaper route, which took him through cavernous apartment buildings in Minneapolis. The buildings were spooky in the predawn hours, but as long as Dad had his dog, he felt safe. Then the dog got sick. Rather than take it to a vet, Margaret enlisted one of her brothers to beat it to death in the basement. She didn't even send Dad away. He listened at the door as the dog yelped and howled and finally fell silent. Mom paused. "Margaret used to say, 'You know, John never liked his paper route after that.' She just didn't get it."

According to Mom, Dad wanted his life to be like a Norman Rockwell painting, which was why he'd married a fresh-faced prom queen from a small town. "I remember we used to drive around to bars looking for Margaret's car. If we saw it, John would go in the back way and try to talk her into going home." He wished for a life of soda fountains, homey Christmases, and kindly old folks. He overestimated how good "good" people were and also how bad were the "bad." The world was divided in two. Even after Dad established the beginnings of the fabled middle-class existence, once he had the wife and kids, he didn't know what to do with us. He didn't know how to fit in.

I knew that everything Mom said was true. The parts of Dad that lived inside me rustled at recognition. Certainly, I'd never beaten anyone, but I shut kids inside their bedrooms when I baby-sat, then turned up the television to mask their cries. These were callous acts. Would I slippery-slope to murder?

The next time I saw Dad, I scooted as far from him as possible on the front seat of the Cadillac, concerned he'd molest me. I'm not sure why that was my particular worry. I looked him over and envisioned him beating Elmer's head. Kicking my mother. Wielding a bloody pipe. When I asked about these episodes, he didn't defend himself. He didn't say anything except, "There are two sides to every story." His answer introduced just enough fuzz to the scenes inhabiting my imagination. That he didn't get angry or ball his fists seemed like a good sign. I'd never fall prey to his temper. This was a line I was sure he wouldn't cross.

It was a hot Friday evening in mid-July 1982. The green house was packed up and practically empty. We'd lugged everything we owned, save our beds and a few necessities—toothbrushes, shampoo—into a yellow moving truck. We'd dined on foil-wrapped hot ham-and-cheese sandwiches from Burger King, as many as we wanted. I stood in the tiny bathroom with my curling iron, creating a frame of curls that rolled straight back from my face. I wore my favorite T-shirt and a pair of Gitano jeans. This was my last night in Watertown and I felt the kind of numbness you feel after an explosion. Except there had been no explosion.

A car pulled up out front and honked. It was my ride to the Dusk 'til Dawn showing at the East Park drive-in. I didn't know what was playing, but it didn't matter. The Dusk 'til Dawn shows were merely an excuse to stay out all night with beer and boys. The wavy terrain of the gravel parking lot, with its muted lighting and distant, sexy voices, was clandestine, romantic. Each backseat was a potential love nest. Tonight, I would drink as much Old Milwaukee, or Miller, or Schlitz as I pleased.

The lot was packed with Chevelles and Firebirds and parents' oversized Oldsmobiles. I made the rounds with my friend Shelly. We talked and flirted and convinced boys to pull cold cans for us from the coolers in their trunks. Then she wandered off and left me with two boys in the backseat of a blue Duster.

There were nods and winks. I tried to pick up on what the signals meant. These were homegrown boys from my neighborhood whom I'd known since grade school. Yet there was something predatory inside them now. I hadn't received much guidance regarding sex. How relationships worked—what was expected from each party— was a mystery to me. Mom showed me how to use maxipads and tampons, but she left the more uncomfortable details to the school and its ridiculous "girls' film." Maybe she didn't consider herself a reliable source on love. Dad gave me only two pieces of advice. He warned me to stay away from "dirty little boys" because they only wanted to "get into my pants." Then, sensing the inevitable, he explained that if I ever wanted to insult a boy, I should never call him an asshole. Boys secretly prided themselves on being assholes.

One of the boys offered me a fresh beer. I swigged heartily from the can and leaned back against the seat. He took my hand, moved in, and kissed me. At first, he kept his lips together. Then, his mouth opened, unleashing a blob of hard tongue that jabbed at my tonsils.

The boy placed my hand on his lap, wrapping my fingers around the newly animated limb sticking out of his fly. It was warm and velvety—not slippery or prosthetic, as I'd imagined—and looked purple in the light. He smirked, his eyes half-closed in exaggerated lustiness. "What do you think?" he asked. I jerked my hand away and huffed out of the car, slamming the door.

He yelled after me. "Teeeeeease! I suppose if I was Fielding it would be different!"

Lanky with bushy blond hair, Fielding was an older boy from the South. I loved his accent and his pointy chin and sly, small mouth. Fielding was my first boyfriend. We used to park his car out in the cornfields and kiss by the glow of the dash. Fielding would come and go from Watertown—I hadn't seen him in months—but, according to the intricate system of messaging at the drive-in, he was supposed to show up tonight.

Shelly found me searching for harbor between rows of cars. She was out of breath: "Fielding's here and he wants to see you!" She led me to a group of boys huddled around a brown Chevy. Fielding was wearing jeans and a button-up shirt; his hands were stuffed into his front pockets.

We necked in the backseat of his car. "I'm sorry you're moving away," he said. "I really like you, you know." He predicted I'd be a knockout once I hit senior high. It was the first time a male other than my father had said I was pretty. He suggested we go to his house.

The house was dark when we arrived. We climbed the stairs to his bedroom and sat on the wooden floor in shadowy light. We laid down and kissed for a long time. "Would you do it with me?" he whispered. "We may never see each other again." I was feeling intensely sorry for myself. My father was a murderer. Tomorrow, I would leave town and never be heard from again. I longed for a threshold, something momentous.

"What if I get pregnant?"

"Well, then we'll get married."

He unzipped my pants and put his hand on my stomach. "It'll be okay," he said. Obviously, he'd done this before. He scooted his jeans down past his narrow hips and got on top. He maneuvered with his hand. Other than pain, I didn't feel anything. It didn't last long.

When I got home, it was nearly sunup. My brother was standing in the kitchen window, still the sentry.

"Where have you been?"

"Out."

"Out with boys?"

"Shut up."

A few hours later, Mom sang from the doorway, "Time to get up! Rise and shine!" Her voice echoed through the empty house. I opened my eyes. Mom looked depressed. Doc was thumping around outside, checking things. His face was red, deep creases forming bands of skin like rubber hoses. When I came out of the bathroom, I felt queasy. Morning sickness, I thought.

We hauled the last of our things to the truck. Then Mom, Nick, Liz, and I took a final walk through the house, bidding farewell to its rooms, to the memories contained within.

"This was a good old house." That was all Mom could choke out.

She plopped the keys on the washing machine and pulled the side door shut for the last time. We'd corralled our pets into the Chevette, save one. We couldn't find our cat, Charlie. Horror set in. Leaving him behind was unthinkable. We pictured him sitting on the deserted porch, waiting. He'd cry little cat cries. Liz pled with Doc to wait for Charlie to show up, but he wouldn't hear of it.

Chop, chop, he said.

10

March and April 1995

Since 1789, U.S. Marshals and their Deputies have answered the call to service of the American people. From taking the census to protecting the President, the missions of the Service have changed to meet the needs of the nation. Today, the Marshals Service is responsible for providing protection for the federal judiciary, transporting federal prisoners, protecting endangered federal witnesses and managing assets seized from criminal enterprises. In addition, the men and women of the Marshals Service pursue and arrest 55 percent of all federal fugitives, more than all other federal agencies combined.

The backbone of the Marshals Service has always been the individual Deputy Marshal. Portrayed throughout history for legendary heroics in the face of lawlessness, these Deputies carry out their daily assignments with dedication and professionalism.

—FROM U.S. MARSHALS SERVICE
PROMOTIONAL MATERIALS

IN ORDER TO "pursue and arrest" my father, the marshals had to create a portrait of who he was. Dad was a chameleon; pinning him down wouldn't be easy.

Certain facts were readily available. They existed in file folders and computer databases in public records offices—points on the government star that shines over us all. In a report entitled "Personal History of Absconder," my father was officially described as follows: John Bryson Vogel; 6'2"; 180 pounds; brown hair; Caucasian; blue eyes; born 10/4/42 in Sauk Centre, Minnesota; both parents deceased; involved in previous criminal activity including two robberies—one armed; no known aliases; no known tattoos; owner of a 1986 brown Oldsmobile Regency four-door sedan, license number 336 CNJ; last seen by his sister on the afternoon of January 22. Occupation: printer.

Also on record was a drunk driving charge, an arrest for disorderly conduct, Dad's marriage to and divorce from Mom (she'd petitioned the court on grounds of "extreme cruelty"), and the existence of three offspring, including one—me—who lived within convenient range of the marshals' District of Minnesota office.

Once they'd determined the basic facts, the marshals issued "Wanted" posters to be dangled from pegs in post offices across the nation. I was unprepared for the sight of my father's face on a "Wanted" poster. For a brief moment I was exhilarated by its blunt impact. He was Jesse James, Clyde Barrow, public enemy number one. Then, as my head settled, I saw my father the way the public, appalled and frightened, saw him. He was the derelict from down the street, an episode of *Cops*. The poster was emblazoned with the bold-type declaration, "Wanted by U.S. Marshals." It included a physical description and the warning, "FUGITIVE SHOULD BE CONSIDERED ARMED AND DANGEROUS."

The poster featured a terrible snapshot of Dad looking every bit the lunatic. Photographed the day after his arrest at the print shop, he appeared disoriented, as though he'd just awakened to discover himself jailed and surrounded by police. His wide owl eyes were shaded by dark, puffy sacks. A rogue lock stuck from his unwashed hair like a horn. His mustache was poorly trimmed, forming a crooked triangle pointing up at his nose. He was wearing an unzipped nylon winter jacket and clutching a pair of sunglasses, along with a tilted placard listing his crime as "counterfeit."

The marshals knew the facts about Dad, but they didn't know his heart. They didn't know, for instance, that he chewed his nails, or that he drank vodka gimlets, or that he preferred brunettes. That he'd come close to sailing around the world and didn't believe in God. This sort of information could have come only from friends and family, who are exactly the people marshals rely on when tracking a fugitive. They choose a starting point from existing data, a first door to knock on, and leapfrog from there. They collect pieces as they go, any bit of information—a name, an address, a cigarette brand, a favorite patch of woods—in order to reconstruct a man's past. People are habitual. From the past is crafted the future.

Marshals are in a tricky position when it comes to divining useful information from people closest to the fugitive. The feds represent court and prison and costly fines. Yet they've got to convince a brother or daughter or close friend that turning in the person he or she loves is the best, perhaps the only option. Agents comfort and assure: *At least in jail your brother or father or close friend will be alive.* They feel around for cracks in relationships. They drive wedges in hopes of obtaining leads and, in the best scenarios, deputizing pseudo-marshals who will act as their eyes and ears.

Agent Kawaters and his partner burned up the phone lines and knocked on doors all across Minnesota. Practically everyone my father knew was updated about his antics, the secret self he'd worked so hard to conceal. The service ferreted out ex-business partners, lovers, bartenders, gun sellers, optometrists, members of an AA group Dad had attended, even a man who bought a car from him ten years prior. On Mother's Day, they staked out Grandma Margaret's grave at St. Vincent cemetery, but my father didn't show. They spoke with the caretaker, flashed a photo. The man said he'd never seen anyone, let alone Dad, visit Grandma's grave.

The search was more confounding than the marshals had anticipated. They began to realize that over the years Dad had whittled down his collection of friends to almost nil. He was estranged from most of his family. He didn't confide in even those to whom he was closest. The police interviewed a friend who'd lunched with Dad at a VFW in the Minneapolis suburb of Edina on the day he'd been arrested. The reaction was familiar. The friend claimed to be "completely shocked" by news of the counterfeiting; Dad had chatted so nonchalantly, mainly about purchasing the Harbor Inn restaurant in northern Minnesota.

Public versions of the official interview reports, which I obtained through the cherished federal Freedom of Information Act, are pocked with large and small black rectangles that blot out details considered private or libelous, including the names of those speaking. Some are almost completely redacted, such as a report taken in February that—after a full page of obliterated text—ends with "[blank] further stated the subject is a loner and an introvert who is a heavy smoker and drinks vodka gimlets."

It's easy enough, however, to identify many of the interviewees by what they said and how they said it. I recognized myself immediately in the transcripts. After several requests, in which I argued that the marshals were hardly required to shield information about me from me, I obtained a mostly unredacted version of an "intelligence update" dated February 22. Reading my statements as perceived by police was unsettling. One quality was evident and quite accurate: steely resentment toward Dad.

Jennifer was cooperative. She stated that she has not seen nor heard from the subject for several years. Jennifer did state that she attempted to establish a relationship with the subject upon his release from federal jail in 1990. However, her attempts lasted for six months and she discontinued any efforts. Jennifer does not "know" her father nor has any desire . . . The subject thinks Jennifer is a cold heartless person. Jennifer does not anticipate the subject contacting her. Jennifer stated that she would have her mother contact this office regarding an interview.

Jennifer was cooperative, however she is employed as a journalist for the City Pages newspaper [blank].

Other reports detail more dead-end interviews. They allude to broken hearts and long-ago farewells and end with promises to call should the unlikely occur and Dad surface for help. One of these reports likely pertains to a conversation with Lloyd, Grandma Margaret's husband from 1971 until her death. Lloyd wore horn-rimmed glasses and tight white T-shirts. He chewed tobacco and proudly displayed a tattoo of a naked woman riding his biceps. He was nice enough, calling Nick "Nickademus" and taking Liz on expeditions to "test the fences" around the farm where he and Grandma lived. More often than not, she came back having been mildly electrocuted.

Lloyd and Dad had clashed from the beginning. There are stories of fistfights, including one that is alleged to have occurred after Lloyd wolfishly chased Cheryl around a kitchen table. Lloyd and Dad parted for good just after Grandma Margaret's funeral. My father was convinced that Lloyd had messed with the will, fixing it so he, Cheryl, and Tom didn't receive their fair shares. Dad even drew Nick, Liz, and me into the fray by claiming that Grandma's original will had provided for our college tuitions. He bragged that he retaliated by ordering fifteen pewter chess sets and charging them to Lloyd's credit card. He chuckled happily as he described this clever revenge. I have the feeling he went further than that.

Lloyd told the marshals that he and the Vogels hadn't been on "friendly terms" since the funeral, "due to the size of their inheritance." He said Dad once borrowed money to bail out a failing real estate business and never repaid it. He didn't know where Dad was, but promised to call if he heard anything.

The marshals tracked Debbie down in Hawaii. She and Dad had stuck together for almost ten years and enjoyed genuinely good times, but I remember my father sitting me down and offering, "If you don't want Debbie around, I'll tell her to leave." The next thing I knew, she was gone, tired of waiting for Dad to make a lasting commitment. "I'll never get married again," he'd told her, implying that his stance was nothing personal. Once, he presented her with a ring. She'd held the velvet box in her palm, thinking that he'd changed his mind, that inside was an engagement band. But it was a cameo instead: pretty, with its ivory-shouldered lady, but pretty disappointing, too—a symbol of the way Dad kept falling short. He drove her to the airport in 1981 and she never saw him again.

Judging by a report that I assume refers to the marshals' conversation with Debbie, she defended Dad the best she could. She told them he was "very intelligent and adept at finding shortcuts and circumventing the system." The marshals tried to lower her estimation a bit. The interviewing officer wrote, "However, when I informed her about the facts of Vogel's counterfeiting operation and how he got caught (U.S. Mail drug dog), she agreed that it did not make much sense."

The one person who might have assisted the marshals—Cheryl, Dad's sister—wouldn't talk. (At least, there are no reports reflecting an interview.) So the police honed in on northern Minnesota. They knew Dad had visited Jimmy just prior to his disappearance, as well as many times before that. They knew about the pending purchase of the Harbor Inn, about the long-ago cabin on Round Lake, and about Dad's fondness for trees and beaches and lawn-chair afternoons. In fact, the police concluded that northern Minnesota "is probably the most likely place VOGEL would choose to re-enter his life, if ever."

They interviewed and reinterviewed Jimmy. Expense reports show that agents made at least two trips to the town where he lived. They discovered that my father had called Jimmy on February 23, a month after vanishing. Jimmy told police the two talked for about five minutes. Dad apologized for involving him in his legal troubles and claimed to need just a little more time before turning himself in. Jimmy tried to talk Dad into surrendering because, according to the interview report, "he did not want to see his friend spend the rest of his life behind bars, but he also stated he did not want to see VOGEL hurt."

The marshals poked around town questioning the owners of car dealerships, checking whether my father had stopped in to trade the Regency for a less conspicuous vehicle. A few salespeople said Dad looked familiar, but none recalled having seen him recently. Nobody had purchased the Olds. The marshals then spoke with the owners of the Harbor Inn, who said they'd talked with Jimmy about the sale, but hadn't received any money. Although the owners had observed Dad at the inn on two occasions in late 1994, neither had actually met him.

As the marshals pieced together the fragments of Dad's character, they wired updates to various law enforcement agencies across the country. One, which went out to marshals in "Every City, USA," described Dad's "personal traits" as follows:

Periodically wears glasses (last known to be wire rimmed
   and silver in color)
Smokes cigarettes (no particular brand)
Drinks alcoholic beverages and will visit social clubs (such
   as a VFW or an American Legion Post), as well as
   neighborhood bars
Socializes with women younger than himself
Utilizes national chain hotels/motels (Best Western, Holiday
   Inn, etc)
Has been previously employed as a real estate broker,
   owner/operator of a printing (offset type) business and
   a traveling salesman (no particular product line)
Pays for services in cash
Counterfeited only $100 bills
In the past, the subject had owned and lived aboard a
   sailboat

From the point of view of the marshals, Dad's most problematic attribute was that he was a loner and therefore difficult to predict. They couldn't stake out a few homes and assume he'd eventually show up at one of them. He could have been traveling in any direction, making for any destination.

Because Dad had mailed the package containing cocaine and counterfeiting supplies from Brownsville, on the border of Mexico, and because he'd refurbished an ocean-worthy sailboat in Florida and obviously enjoyed traveling, the police thought he might attempt to flee the country. A late February memo listed "suspected location" as "Europe, Caribbean, Canada, Mexico . . . investigation indicates financial activity in the U.K. and the Bahamas." The marshals had obtained one of Dad's address books, which was plump with Mexican phone numbers and names. Next to cryptic entries like "Sodium Hydroxide, international chemical co." and "eagles on the border" were addresses for places such as "de los ojos cafe." A Spanish lesson book had been found among his possessions at the print shop.

The marshals posted photos of Dad at various border crossings. They made "lane inquiries" but found no record of his car having entered the United States from Canada or Mexico. Mexico doesn't inspect entrants too closely. Dad could have slipped south unnoticed. The inquiries also assumed he was still driving the Olds.

On April 17, the marshals interviewed a man claiming to know where Dad was hiding. Because the man's story involved a Mexican border town, the lead seemed especially promising. According to this man, whose identity and relationship to my father are redacted from police reports, he heard Dad's name mentioned in January over a channel on his police scanner. He called a phone number and spoke with a woman who promised to relay Dad a message. My father returned the man's call during the first week of February and demanded that he travel immediately to Brownsville. The man did as told, flying alone to the Brownsville airport, where he and Dad met up. They drove in a rented gray Dodge Intrepid and stayed at a hotel on "the strip" called the New Frontier.

My father was uncomfortable and jumpy in Brownsville, so the two drove to the Mexican border and walked across into Matamoros. Dad used a fake ID, possibly a Texas driver's license. While in Mexico, Dad asked to borrow $50,000 in order to "alter his appearance" and begin a new enterprise counterfeiting American, Spanish, and Canadian currency. He bragged of already possessing the necessary Treasury seals. The bulk of their trip to Mexico, however, was spent purchasing trinkets and pharmaceuticals from the Farmacia de Panama. The man returned from the trip to Brainerd via Continental Airlines.

Raising the $50,000 Dad asked for proved impossible. The man's father wouldn't make the loan. In the end, he was able to lay his hands on a mere $1,500 by maxing out his own credit cards. With the funds, he headed back to Matamoros. During this second trip, he utilized an agreed-upon code in order to notify my father of his presence: He showed up at the Farmacia de Panama, placed a specific order, and "somehow Vogel would know he was there and appear." All told, he crossed the border to see Dad approximately ten times.

The marshals tried to verify the man's story. They checked car rental records and found that "the mileage supports the statements made by [blank]. Additionally, the type of vehicle and rental agreement coincides with the data supplied by [blank]." A friend of the informant corroborated the bit about the police scanner, saying he was in the car with the man when Dad's name was broadcast. The friend remembered the man saying he knew my father and rushing to look up a phone number in his address book. He also said he witnessed the phone call.

In early May, the man was asked to submit to a polygraph examination. The test, administered at the FBI office in Minneapolis, lasted two hours and was "extremely difficult," according to police reports, due to the man's "excitable and erratic behavior." The result was clear enough, though: he'd been lying all along. "As a result of this exam, all leads generated by [blank] have been halted . . . The polygraph examiner stated that although [blank] probably traveled to Brownsville, Texas and Matamoros, Mexico . . . [blank] never really met Vogel at all."

11

Also in April 1995

"Excuse me. Is your father a thief?"

I was leaning against a long, polished bar in Kansas City, about to gather whiskey drinks for myself and my sister. I examined the face, the dark brown eyes of the smiling man before me, seeking hint of recognition or motive. *How does he . . . All the way in Kansas City, how in the fuck does he know?* My knees threatened to buckle. My head turned to melted wax.

"Because he must have stolen the stars from the sky and put them in your eyes."

A pickup line. The worst ever. Delivered at the worst moment ever to the worst person ever.

Out of sheer relief, I lurched to my toes. Happy, high, and still anonymous, I grabbed the two glasses and slipped past the lady killer. I made my way back toward the table where Liz waited. She was perched like a young Bette Davis, her elbow on the table, puffing on a cigarette. Her thin, stately nose and intelligent eyes lent her a commanding demeanor. She'd always been the sort others strive to please and impress, which is fortunate because she fields disappointment hard.

Liz and I had arrived in Kansas City the day before, having driven down in her beat-up Pontiac Sunbird. One of her sculptures—an enameled pin shaped like a pod with curlicue bugs crawling from it—had been chosen for display at a moderately prestigious art show in Topeka, sixty miles away. Liz can draw and sculpt as skillfully as Dad, sometimes creating those same fine, realistic faces. Mostly, though, her pieces are abstract.

We'd checked into the hotel just before sundown and requested a room on the top floor. It boasted a panoramic view of downtown, which, frankly, wasn't much to boast about. Aside from some patches of green grass and a red-roofed church, the city appeared gray and featureless. Our room had two double beds. I chose the one on the left. Then, overtaken by an exuberant fit, I began leaping up and down on the bed, still wearing heavy boots. It caved under the pressure.

I hopped to the floor and examined the sinkhole at the center of the mattress. "Oh shit! We're going to get charged for that!"

"No, we won't." Liz remained calm, sensible. "Just call downstairs and say we want another room."

God raised an eyebrow and cleared His throat. I was gripped by fear. "I can't do that. I can't call downstairs and say that."

Liz picked up the phone. "Hi. We've got a little problem. One of our beds isn't very comfortable and we'd like another room." She smiled at me. "It appears to be sagging."

She replaced the receiver. "No problem. They're moving us down the hall."

I considered propping up the bed with a garbage can, rendering the mattress pothole less noticeable, but then thought better of it. A garbage can would evidence a cover-up.

Early next morning, continental breakfasts in hand, we set off for Topeka. We easily located the hall where Liz's pin was on display. Milling about, we assessed the competition, snorting at gaudy glass art and admiring select paintings and metal sculptures. We carried ourselves like the women of exquisite taste we believed ourselves to be.

On the way back to Kansas City, I suggested a tour of legendary Leavenworth penitentiary, the original "big house," which sits just northeast of Topeka. Prisons fascinate me. Many of my favorite movies involve the heroic, or at least charming, efforts of a miscon-strued crook who gets sent to the joint: *Cool Hand Luke, Good-Fellas, Papillon, Escape from Alcatraz, Down by Law, The Shawshank Redemption.* Because I understand the difficulty in being straight among a curvy and pretzel-twisted world, I root for bad guys.

Leavenworth is wide and squat, with endless rows of tiny square windows facing the parking lot. It's constructed of fine tan stone and surrounded by a mammoth chain-link fence topped with scrambles of razor wire. Over the front entrance, marking the cen-ter of the institution, sits a large, shiny dome.

Liz and I trotted up the steps and opened the door. We stood before a Plexiglas booth where a heavyset man was finishing a sandwich.

I spoke first. "Hi. We're wondering if we can take a tour of the prison."

The man smiled and placed his crust on a piece of waxed paper. "I'm very sorry, ladies, but all tours have to be prearranged due to security concerns. We do background checks and so forth."

"You're kidding. You couldn't make an exception? We've come a long distance."

"The only other way to get inside these walls is to be convicted of a crime."

A second man—taller, bald—leaned in and added, "That's right, ladies. You have to be indicted to be invited!"

We laughed joyously, the four of us, the matter of my request having been settled by this unexpected bit of gallows humor.

The clerk at our hotel had recommended this crummy club, festooned with brass rails and inhabited by a slick, middle-aged clientele. "Great jazz," he'd said, passing us a slip of paper. In the 1920s and '30s, Kansas City was considered America's jazz capital. Notably, said the clerk, this was the birthplace of Charlie Parker. Things seemed to have degenerated since the halcyon days. I reached the table where Liz sat waiting just as the mediocre trum-pet player peeled off a cranium-splitting solo.

"God, that guy is awful." I handed Liz her whiskey-and-seven. "He ought to be arrested for playing like that."

"Yes," Liz replied, "indicted and invited."

We laughed and clinked our glasses together in a toast.

"It's strange about Dad, isn't it." Liz lit another cigarette.

"Yeah, I keep wondering where he is."

"I wonder too." Liz's eyes grew wide, her manner confidential. "Isn't it amazing? All we've been through. People wouldn't believe it if we told them."

"I know. Sometimes I fantasize about just blurting it out. All of it."

Our conversation was governed by detached marvel. It had been so long since either of us had spoken to Dad that we perceived him in abstract, purely psychological terms—a substitute, I suppose, for abject horror. We'd analyzed why he'd turned out the way he had. We'd established the principles that guided him. We'd discussed intelligence, charm, and whether he'd gone insane, as smart people sometimes do. Dad was also a mine shaft we raided for clues about ourselves. Liz and I had uncovered ways in which we were like one another and, in turn, like Dad. As Liz put it, he'd bequeathed to us the ability to "see through things." See ugliness, I supposed. In our most charitable moments, we attributed to Dad whatever modicum of sophistication we might possess.

Two young men—college types, judging by their baggy jeans and smooth faces—approached our station at the back of the bar. They sat down and initiated small talk, inquiring about our schooling, our jobs, where we were from. They asked all manner of perfunctory questions, until they got around to wondering what our father did for a living. Liz and I looked at each other, our thoughts catching like a finely tuned trapeze act.

She said it. "He's a counterfeiter."

The words sounded completely absurd. The men fell silent. Waiting. "She's serious. He's on the lam right now. The police can't find him anywhere."

The blond sporting the backward baseball cap looked from Liz to me and then to Liz again. He thought he recognized a joke. He grinned widely, then threw his head back and let out a howl. We laughed too.

A waitress brought another round of drinks. In less than an hour, she'd track the four of us sleuthlike to a neighboring bar, where we'd go without settling the bill. She'd interrupt my attempt at landing the nine ball in the corner pocket. In her apron, with a pen behind her ear, she'd wave the white ticket. It would take a minute to recognize her.

I arrived home, at my Minneapolis apartment, with a throbbing headache. I dragged my duffel upstairs and clicked on the TV. I pulled open the refrigerator and hit the button on the answering machine. There was a message from one of the marshals, Kawaters's partner. "Hi, Jennifer. This is Fred Flintstone. Say, when this is all over, I was wondering if maybe we could go out."

I was furious. The call was either a lame attempt at winning my confidence or a grave misconstruction of our relationship. Did Fred think I was on his side? Did he really believe that after throwing Dad in the slammer, we'd catch a movie? It struck me that perhaps I'd been too friendly, given the wrong impression. To clear up any confusion, I phoned the agent's supervisor and lodged a complaint. He never came to my house again.

Saturdays were for Simonizing

12

THE NICE HOUSE we were promised in Cedar Rapids turned out to be a sparsely furnished dwelling in a run-down part of town; it was a white-sided nightmare. Cedar Rapids itself was ugly and industrial, with no detectable soul. Officially, it was billed the City of Five Seasons (the fifth being the "time to enjoy"), but everyone called it the City of Five Smells because it stunk from every direction.

Mom and Doc drank constantly, locked in slow, lugubrious competition. Doc was prone to passing out while cooking, leaving pans of lutefisk to char on the stovetop, and wearing loose-fitting boxers and no pants so that his chicken-skin balls hung out. He resented my family more each day because he'd abandoned his wife and kids and social standing on our behalf and because he loathed the meatpacking plant. Apparently his employees loathed him as well because more than once after finishing a shift, he came outside to find long key strokes in the paint of his big, blue New Yorker.

Doc's transformation was remarkable. There were no glazed donuts or Poe readings in Cedar Rapids. Instead, he woke us early on Saturdays for chores. Resistance served merely as evidence of our lazy natures. Standing outside in his bathrobe with a mixed drink in his hand, he held court while we Simonized his car to a high shine. With each cocktail, his face grew more stern and his complaints more emphatic. He said that we were spoiled rotten. We were not children, but rather drains on his bank account.

Doc regularly commented on my breasts. I'd come downstairs, dressed for school, and he'd call out, "Why, I think your boobs are getting as big as your mother's!" I woke one night to discover him in bed with me, drunk to the point of palsy. Mom stood in the doorway, trying to coax him out. She said, "Come on, you're in the wrong bed," like it was a mistake. It seemed to me, however, that a person doesn't take a left at the end of the hall every night for months and then suddenly, accidentally, take a right. I began spending a lot of time away from the house.

I stayed with friends, bad girls with ruined families. Sometimes I was away for days. I cruised the city's main drag in my friend Michelle's white Pinto listening to AC/DC and scouting for parties. I stole bottles of Doc's Black Velvet and peppermint schnapps and huffed bowls of pot. One evening, stoned, I locked the keys inside the Chevette with the engine running and the headlights blazing. I simply went to my room and closed the door.

For the first time in my life, I did poorly in school. A counselor could have hatched all kinds of theories about neglect and what happens when a fifteen-year-old girl is uprooted from her hometown, but the most tangible reason for my academic nosedive was that I was popping large amounts of speed, which made it impossible to concentrate. Speed afforded me bravery. I ditched classes, spending the better part of each day smoking cigarettes and joints in back of Thomas Jefferson High with the other stoners and delinquents.

I was learning a particular sort of independence. It was gradual at first. But then, all at once, I realized that nothing terrible happened when I broke the rules. I could allow bells to ring all around and not budge. I lost the desire to do what was requested or required of me. I said no over and over again. Sometimes I said nothing at all, declining to fill silence. The more resolute I became, the less I spoke. The less I spoke, the more I was convinced I had nothing to say.

Mom didn't appreciate this newfound, if skewed, autonomy. She couldn't get me to stay home or answer questions like "What's wrong with you?" All I could think was, Mom's life was in ruins, so she had no grounds on which to dictate the details of mine.

One afternoon she and I had a terrible fight. I don't remember how it started, but I do recall firing off an arsenal of accusations. Silence split apart and out spattered bile. My mother wasn't my mother anymore. She was just a woman. I pointed out her drinking, the less attractive aspects of Doc, the charade of their relationship. She called me an alley cat and said I was throwing my life away. We bandied how-dare-yous and well-look-at-yous, and the volume kept increasing. The argument reached its apex when I called my mother a slut. If I'd forgotten the line not to be crossed, Mom hadn't. She grabbed me by the hair and threw me out onto the porch, locking the door behind me.

I swore I'd never again set foot inside that house, and I didn't, except to gather some clothes and cassette tapes. A few days after my grand departure, Michelle dropped me around the corner. The plan was that I would slip into and out of the house without detection. As I approached, though, I saw Mom and Liz sitting on the front steps. They looked grim.

"I've come to get a few of my things. I won't be long."

Neither Mom nor Liz spoke.

I walked past them into the house, thinking Mom might reach out and grab my ankle. But she didn't. I went upstairs and opened the door to the bedroom I shared with Liz. Though I'd been away only a short time, the room looked and felt very different, like a skin I'd shed. I quickly packed my belongings into a large black garbage bag. Liz came in and perched on her bed.

"Where are you going to live?"

"I've got friends I can stay with."

We were silent for a few minutes. Liz looked small and helpless.

The thought of leaving her behind to endure Mom and Doc tore me up. But Nick would look after her, I was sure. "I'm really sorry to leave you here. I just have to go. I can't stay."

"It's okay." Liz looked as though she might cry. "I understand."

I finished packing, then I hugged Liz and threw the garbage bag over my right shoulder, making for the door.

We were peas in a pod

13

MY FATHER WAS waiting at the bus terminal when I hopped down off the Greyhound from Cedar Rapids, black garbage bag in tow. He'd paid for the ticket, just as he'd mailed me $100 every month since I'd left Mom's, keeping me in Marlboros and hot lunches. When I'd called to explain what had happened, he'd sounded genuinely pleased that I wanted to move to Minneapolis. I remember what he said: "Of course, honey. I've always wanted you to live with me. You know that."

Still, I was apprehensive. I'd spent summers and birthdays with Dad, but this was different. I was asking for stability, reliability, a warm bed and unexpired cartons of milk. All these years, my father had avoided the pedestrian travails of parenthood—chicken pox and boils and heartbroken daughters who flee school lunchrooms in tears. He was unaccustomed to being inconvenienced. He'd never had to weigh permissible behavior, enforce rules, say "no, you can't."

I was relieved that he wanted me and I hoped the fact of me wouldn't change his mind. But then, so what if it did. I'd simply strike out on my own again. I could take care of myself.

Since leaving Mom's, my taste for independence had grown sharper. I'd spent the last two months bouncing from one friend's basement to the next, doing exactly as I pleased while still finishing tenth grade. Pitying parents shared their dinner tables. The most accommodating couple allowed me to stay for nearly three weeks in their daughter's bedroom. One morning before school, I convinced the daughter to get soused on lime vodka. With the door closed, we curled our hair and sang along with the radio, "We're gonna rock down to Electric Avenue, and then we'll take it higher!" We even packaged shots to go in tiny Tupperware containers. I handled the drunk pretty well, but she threw up on her desk in homeroom. When her parents said I was a bad influence and had to go, I didn't argue.

Dad swung the Cadillac into a parking spot near a large tan garage, part of the Westbrook town house complex.

"I've got everything set up. I moved into this place last month. You can have the whole basement to yourself. That way you'll have some privacy. A girl your age needs privacy."

"You didn't have to go to all that trouble."

"Nothing's too good for my number-one daughter." He threw the transmission into park and switched off the engine. "By the way, I've got a surprise for you."

Dad exited the car, long legs first, and lifted the garage door. Inside, like Cleopatra rolled in the rug, was a Fiat Spider convertible with the top down.

"It was orange when I bought it, but I had it painted red for you. Convertibles should be red, don't you think?" He was running his hand along the car's back end. "Why don't you hop in?"

I was stunned. I opened the door and slid onto the driver's seat. My eyes darted from the glossy wooden dash to a panel of elegant meters, then to the racing-style steering wheel emblazoned in the center with the Fiat emblem. I'd never been so near anything so fine. I said, "Wow." It wasn't a short, bursting *wow*, but a long, drawn-out one. A *wow* with steam coming off it.

"It's Italian. It should go pretty good."

"Dad, thank you so much! Is it really mine?"

"Sure. A girl your age needs her own wheels. Now, just a few rules. I only want you to drive it during the day and only when I know where you're going and when you'll be back."

"No problem, Dad. No problem."

The car was a bribe. He may as well have fallen to his knees and pleaded, *Love me!* It was only the first day and already he'd placed himself at a disadvantage. He wouldn't judge me. In fact, he antici- pated that I would do the judging. The car meant Dad wasn't pre- pared for an authoritarian role. I knew this, just as I knew that the rule about driving only during the day wouldn't stick. I swiveled on the leather seat to face him. "I should have moved in with you a long time ago."

My father stuffed his hands into his pockets and stood in the driveway beaming.

The town house was minimally furnished. There was an earth- toned sofa and love seat arranged in an L, the glass dining table from the Brainerd cabin, a shelf that held a television and a meager book collection (various how-to manuals, a Rockwell retrospective, and Sir Richard Burton's *The Erotic Traveler,* page-marked with a Chinese cookie fortune that promised "Your love life will be happy and fulfilling"), a couple of wall hangings that Debbie had stitched years prior, and ashtrays.

The basement had no windows, but Dad had provided a ceramic lamp that infused the beige carpeting with a warm glow. He'd also installed a king-size waterbed that occupied nearly half the room. It was made up with a jungle-print sheet and bedspread set and crowned by a clunky wooden headboard with two sliding doors. There was a Fisher stereo with speakers the size of cup- boards, and a clothes rack where I could hang my blouses and jeans. Dad had made an effort and I, generally expecting little from adults, considered it a stroke of honest love and generosity.

Unpacking in my room, I could hear the faint sounds of revving engines and honking horns emanating from the Hopkins strip, which sat less than a mile from Westbrook. Hopkins, it turned out, boasted one of the best cruising stretches in the entire Minneapolis area. The distant, chaotic melody of other people's good times sank me. I turned off the lamp and listened in the dark, floating and bobbing on the waterbed like a message in a bottle.

I wondered whether people rescued from house fires sometimes wished they'd burned with their possessions. I didn't miss Cedar Rapids or Watertown, exactly. I missed familiarity, a world larger than the claustrophobic one in my head.

Dad put on a suit and tie and left the house every weekday morning at ten. He returned at three or four smelling of liquor. I knew he spent the better part of his days at a businessman's bar called Jennings, but I didn't say anything. The bills were being paid and I could see that being a father, even a poor imitation of one, was crucially important to Dad. He'd been granted a purpose and was trying like hell to set a good example. Finally, he'd found an altruistic goad to lying.

Dad actually did have a job at the time. He owned a company called Jarco Home Services, which built, installed, and removed "For Sale" signs for local real estate companies. The trunk of his car was puzzle-fitted with signposts, but they were always the same signposts. There wasn't much turnover in his stock.

Jarco was only the most recent in a long line of entrepreneurial endeavors. Dad had previously owned a franchise of the Lectroglaz corporation, which refinished bathtubs; according to an ex–business partner, Dad had installed a flimsy finish and sold the franchise just before the complaints poured in. He'd also owned a company called Economy Foam Insulation and, of course, the drive-in restaurant near the Annandale farm and RED Inc., the real estate company with the clever pens.

Dad had never been interested in the slow, dutiful mechanics of becoming successful—only in the serene, wrapped-in-cashmere end result. The way he saw it, you were either a garbage collector or a CEO. He was too impatient. He couldn't fathom how people slaved away for years, slowly building equity in their homes, putting their kids through college, saving up for retirement. No, success was a fruit to be plucked and devoured. Dad cut corners and took advantage of people. Each of his businesses was a charade, a box of snake oil he had to unload before his customers wised up, before they rubbed their eyes and realized that the well-heeled charmer they were following was merely John Vogel, cheat; John Vogel, coward; John Vogel, nobody. He tugged and pulled at the nooses he constructed until they slipped away, occasionally catching the necks of those nearby. Then he kicked the ground and pleaded with the sky, Is this all there is?

The only substance sticky and solid enough to patch the hole in Dad, to stave off the constant draining of his self-confidence, was success. And success was measured in terms of money. Money meant a person was important, above reproach. Money equaled peace and happiness. Who could blame him for the mistake? In America, it's practically true.

Once Dad told me, "There are only two kinds of people in this world, givers and takers. Find yourself a giver and you'll have it made." He was ostensibly offering romantic advice, but I've come to understand this bit of wisdom differently. What he really meant was, there are only two kinds of people in this world, those who are doing the screwing and those who are getting screwed. Givers were suckers. And though my father, deep down, believed himself a giver, he had no intention of behaving like one.

There were enemies. When the phone rang at Westbrook, Dad rarely answered it. If I picked up the receiver and the call was for him, I knew to take a message. Though Dad was almost always home, he was never home. Just before sunset each evening, he wheeled about the town house in a maniacal ritual of shade pulling. He was uneasy, hiding out, yet trying mightily to maintain that air of legitimacy. It didn't elude me that his bills were mostly in other people's names or variations on his own, like Bryson Vogel and John Johnson.

One afternoon, my father introduced me to the invention that was going to make him a millionaire. He kept the prototype in the laundry room, which was adjacent to my bedroom in the basement. He pulled it out from behind the door and raised it up for inspection.

"It's a jean stretcher."

"A what?"

"A jean stretcher. It makes jeans longer."

"Really?" The stretcher was constructed of two pieces of plastic pipe threaded together. There was an oarlock at one end and two slits cut into the pipe at the other.

"Sure. You know how my jeans are always a little too short? I buy them long enough and then the washer shrinks them up. There must be other people out there with the same problem."

Dad asked me to retrieve a pair of jeans for a demonstration. He placed the oarlock at the crotch and hooked the pant leg bottoms into the slits. Then he twisted the pipes so they threaded out longer.

"Of course, the jeans should be wet."

"Hmmm. Yeah, I see how that could work."

"Oh, it works, all right. I use it all the time!" He pointed toward the hems of his Wranglers, which fell just at the tops of his loafers.

His enthusiasm made me want to cry. He completely misunderstood what society might accept from him.

Dad advertised the stretcher in the local newspaper, under the company name Voco Products. He designed the ad, which featured a doodle of an unhappy man with short pants next to a happy man with long pants. He offered his invention for $12.95 (or two for $25). I suppose it was possible that there were stilt-legged beanpoles out there who'd never heard of Levi's and that my father received and deposited a handful of checks. But I know for a fact that he never built another jean stretcher. Then he kicked the ground and pleaded with the sky, Is this all there is?

We didn't rely on Dad's inventions or businesses for food and shelter. Grandma Margaret had died in April 1983, just a few months before I'd moved to Minneapolis, and left a small inheritance. It wasn't the settlement she'd intended—Dad still blamed her husband, Lloyd—but it was enough that Dad didn't have to worry about money for a while.

Grandma's death weighed on my father. His shoulders sloped and he watched increasing amounts of television. Grandma hadn't been much of a shield, but she'd been something—a body, an idea. Now he stood on the Vogel family frontline, ready to take a bullet for the next generation. "I won't live past fifty," he said, leaning against the sink holding a dish towel as I scrubbed a frying pan. "None of us do. We all die young, mostly from heart attacks. I've got a heart murmur, did you know that? You've got one too." Grandma was sixty-three when she died of cardiac arrest. Her brother Warren had been forty-seven. And Dad was right, I did have a heart murmur.

It was obvious that Dad's drinking was on the wax. He kept a bottle of vodka on top of the refrigerator, in plain view to signify he didn't have a problem. He'd been ticketed for drunk driving in May, just a month after his mother's heart attack. I expect he'd been drunk since the funeral, when he'd made a splendid entrance by stumbling over a chair in the back row. Sadness filled him like wet sand; when he tripped, it felt like slapstick and he almost laughed. I watched with a cool eye. I knew how careless Grandma had been and I didn't feel particularly sorry that she was dead. I didn't feel anything save concern that I didn't feel anything.

At the funeral home, there was a rest room near the front for especially distraught mourners in need of immediate privacy. My cousin and I ducked in for a chat.

I stared at myself in the mirror. "This is weird. I don't know what to do."

"Did you see how loaded John is?" My cousin seemed amused, as detached as I was.

She inquired as to whether I smoked pot.

After the service, the two of us joined some kids in a square blue car. We drove around Osseo, Minnesota, passing a joint until I was fully transformed into an omnipotent authority on hypocrisy.

What a farce! Somebody should have gotten up at the funeral and described the kind of mother Grandma Margaret truly was! My cousin and I were about to enter Cheryl's house, where Dad and company were hashing over good times, when my cousin caught sight of my face in the harsh porch light. "Oh my God! Look at your eyes!" They were red slits. She said if anyone noticed, I should say I'd been crying. I was repulsed by the suggestion to lie. *Isn't that just like a Vogel!* Yet I knew if anybody had noticed my eyes, I would have claimed tears. Just like a Vogel.

My father and I lolled foot bottom to foot bottom on the sofa and love seat in the living room of the Westbrook town house, every shade carefully and completely drawn. Dad had slow-cooked a nice batch of pepper steak in the electric frying pan and I'd constructed a cheesecake with canned cherries on top. Stuffed, we were watching the end of a *Hill Street Blues* episode in which two cops grill a murder suspect who has multiple personalities. It was a satisfying father/daughter evening, one of those nights where we pledged allegiance to each other.

I was seeing Dad clearly for the first time. He was no longer camouflaged by baby ducks and Christmas trees, by the pretty little veil of childhood admiration. His cynicism, his insecurity, his dishonesty, the sadness at the middle of it all—the threads that crisscrossed his soul were glaring. They were familiar in my bones. We were refugees in a lifeboat, bound together.

Dad mashed out his cigarette and trotted upstairs, returning a few moments later with a large manila envelope. He perched on the edge of the sofa and opened it, removing a short stack of photographs. He could hardly keep the grin off his face.

"What? What are they?"

"Just look."

He passed me the stack. I paged through the pictures. They were family photos—images of Dad and Tom and Cheryl with Grandma

Margaret and Joe. They looked strange. The angles and lighting were off; the shadow from one nose cast left while the shadow from another cast right. It appeared as though the children's torsos had been grafted Frankenstein-style against the shoulders and chests of their parents.

As I fumbled for something complimentary to say, Dad interrupted, explaining that a few weeks prior he'd submitted some old photos to a local restoration shop. He'd paid the shop to combine the images into family portraits of a family that had never existed. Maybe he thought the portraits afforded a glimpse of his life idealized, a rewritten history in which his father hadn't left. Maybe he was trying to reconcile the different versions of who he was.

Slowly, I handed the pictures back. Dad looked at me with tears in his eyes and I knew why he was so happy to have me living in the basement.

A few months into eleventh grade and I was failing, even the classes I attended. I'd only narrowly averted a fistfight with a bruiser named Hillary. What's more, my small-town idea of beauty (big hair, blue eye shadow) didn't play well in the suburbs. On the upside, I'd acquired two new best friends: Jennifer and Anita. The three of us evolved intricate, all-consuming philosophies. We loathed Ronald Reagan and pitied rich people. We shared disdain for hypocrisy and never tired of divining it in teachers, school rules, and society at large. We ditched classes and drank and smoked pot and congratulated ourselves on our honesty.

Dad loathed my new friends. He liked neither their clothes— flannel shirts and old jeans with pen scribbles on them—nor their rebellious attitudes. He complained that they traipsed through our town house like they owned the place, helping themselves to whatever was in the fridge. They didn't say "yes, sir" or "thank you, sir." They disturbed the sanctuary of his slump. My father suggested that I search higher up the social ladder. When I explained that Jennifer and Anita were the best friends I'd ever had, that they *understood* me, he said that what I really needed in the long run were friends who understood success.

In Hopkins, with my Fiat and king-size waterbed and newly honed skepticism, I'd discovered a life where every penny didn't count. I took chances, dug deep to nurture tiny bits of character. I ceased compulsively cleaning. Finally, I got some sleep. This new life came at the expense of the old one. I pretended as though Cedar Rapids had never happened and my mother, brother, and sister didn't exist. I didn't write to them or talk about them. I was the lone gunslinger, the mystery girl with no name. I forgot, moved on, closed my heart. This ability to be cold and blank about people—I'd perfected it as a child, each time I left Dad's house for Mom's or Mom's for Dad's. I used to cry and cry and cry until one day, once and for all, I'd stopped.

When my father told me Nick and Liz were coming for a visit, I acted indifferent. When they arrived, quiet and blond (often, the two had been mistaken for twins), I showed them to my room and said they could play my records, sleep in my bed, even smoke my bong if they wished. Then, due to an awful clawing in my stomach, the familiar urge to repair what was wrong, I deserted them. As I bolted up the stairs, leaving my brother and sister tentative and alone on the edge of my bed, I swelled with the kind of love reserved for fellow soldiers. I kept running because I thought they wanted something from me.

The next afternoon, my father was sipping gimlets and preparing an extravagant meal for the four of us to share around the glass dining table. This was a rare event: Dad and I hardly ever used the table, our meals instead gobbled in front of the television, which seemed to aid his digestion. He marinated steaks and sliced fresh mushrooms, but there was no pepper. "Where the hell is the god-damned pepper?" he growled, fumbling through the cupboard. He got into his Cadillac and headed for the strip mall a few blocks away. As he approached the grocery mart, he saw a black man strolling with a white woman down the sidewalk in broad daylight. My father, on the verge of providing an expensive, delicious meal for his three children, feeling paternal, even righteous, veered onto the curb and tried to strike the black man with his front bumper. "Go back to Africa!" he hollered and sped off.

Dad's hatred for blacks was so virulent that my family had spent countless hours theorizing about its roots. There were suppositions that he'd been beaten or even raped by a black man while in prison for the convenience-store holdups. Others thought his racism originated in childhood, from the moment he was rejected by his supremely handsome German father. Maybe he simply needed to feel superior to somebody. His hatred toward blacks seemed directly proportional to his hatred toward himself.

My father returned to the town house in a lather, his jaw muscles spastic. After he mumbled something to fourteen-year-old Nick about unfinished business, the two set out on foot toward the store.

By the time they arrived, the Hopkins police were already on the scene. Dad, in his agitated and mildly drunk state, assuming, perhaps, that because the officers were white they would automatically side with him, marched confidently toward the small congregation of lights and people. Nick hung back, having been ignored when he'd suggested that the two keep moving.

Dad was arrested and placed in the backseat of a squad car. He called for Nick, tried to wave him over, but Nick turned his back and returned home. The three of us were now alone and would remain so until Monday, when Dad would be released from jail. I showed Nick where Dad kept his pot pipe, barely hidden in his bedroom closet, among sock balls, passports, and occasional cocaine packets. I retrieved the vodka bottle from the top of the refrigerator and poured drinks. We lounged on the furniture—loaded, even little Liz—playing the stereo and thinking life certainly was strange. Just for that night, it was once again the three of us against the world.

On Monday, my father came home in crumpled clothes, hung over. When he sipped from the cocktail he mixed (which amounted to a water gimlet because we'd refilled the vodka bottle from the tap), he gritted his teeth. When, upstairs, he realized that his pot had been raided as well, he railed at us about the importance of privacy. It takes real nerve to scold your children for smoking your pot and drinking your vodka, especially just after you've been arrested for trying to kill a man, but he was still our father, after all.

Dad wasn't a demanding parent. Mostly, he expected that I show a modicum of respect (beginning with staying out of his stash) and share dinner with him a couple of nights a week. It was crucial to him that I not drift away completely. He could forgive almost any transgression, but he wouldn't stand for being shut out. I was allowed to go anywhere, return home at any hour, as long as I was tucked cozily against the belly of my waterbed in the morning.

My father believed in an idealized version of me. He held the same illusions about me that he expected me to hold about him. Fooling him was easy, because he was so willing to fool himself. He was unaware that I skipped classes every day. He had no idea I sold pot to my classmates or drank booze in a van parked in the front lot of the school; nor did he know about the bacchanalian events that took place in my bedroom. Dad kept his word regarding privacy. He hardly ever descended the stairs to the basement. Instead, he called from the doorway and waited as I spastically showered the air with deodorant and stumbled up. At least in the basement I was safe from the world, he figured, a place he patently mistrusted because it was full of people just like him.

Sometimes, when I was in my room with friends, Molly, Dad's girlfriend, would sneak down for a bong hit. Short, almost dwarfish, with a head that appeared too large for her body, Molly was mostly Irish with a wide smile. The first time I met her, she hugged me and winked and, like the big sister I never had, demonstrated the method by which she styled her blond hair; it involved hot rollers and sheets of hair spray. Molly was seven or eight years younger than Dad and regarded him as an old fuster one had to circumvent in order to have any fun. She locked him out of the town house; he splintered the doorjambs to get back in. She sped away in her car; he snapped off the door handle trying to stop her.

Molly would sit cross-legged on the carpeting, inhaling mightily from the bong. She'd exhale and cough and smile that big, shiny smile of hers. With a glint in her eye, she'd groan conspiratorially, "Oh boy, is John in a mood tonight." Then she'd borrow a bud or two with the intent of getting him high. She'd rush back up before he awoke from his nap or returned to the television from the loo.

One day, Molly bestowed upon me a collection of records perfectly preserved from her teenage years. It included Led Zeppelin's *II, III, IV,* and *Physical Graffiti;* the Beatles' *Rubber Soul, Revolver,* and the White Album; the Rolling Stones' *Between the Buttons, Some Girls,* and *Sticky Fingers;* Bob Dylan's *Blood on the Tracks* and *Another Side of Bob Dylan;* Simon and Garfunkel's *Bridge over Troubled Water;* and Janis Joplin's *Pearl.* I played one after the other, over and over. The albums sounded genuine emotions. Just as they once must have for Molly, they captured the dourness of my abiding mood.

The world was fucked, its priorities ludicrous. At school, I started fires. I'd hide in a stall in the girls' bathroom until everyone had cleared out; then I'd drop a lighted paper towel into the giant garbage barrel full of paper towels. I'd get most of the way down the hall before the black cloud billowed from the bathroom. More than once, the top floor of the school had to be evacuated. Fires were simple, so beautifully destructive, and yet so easy to get away with due to the lag time between ignition and full-blown flames. I could see why Dad was always burning things down.

About halfway through the school year, word circulated that a boy named Rob was hosting a cocaine party. Rob supplied most of Hopkins High, and the party promised to be an unprecedented "blowout." That Saturday night, my friends and I pulled up to a landscaped rambler and were personally greeted at the door, Rob's way of regulating the influx of people while at the same time taking orders for coke. He pointed the way to a wood-paneled basement, the central fixture of which was a pool table covered by a tremendous mirror. All around it, people sat on chairs and bar stools, straws up their noses, sucking on long white stripes of powder.

I wasn't a novice. With a razor blade, I adeptly chopped rocks into dust and scraped piles into lines. I sucked up the first hit through a plastic straw and felt the balloon expand in my head. I took another. As I bent down to inhale a third, I caught myself smiling in the mirror. The face didn't look like mine, yet it did. I glanced around the room at the Budweiser sign on the wall, the people laughing and snorting. Everything gleamed with a shimmering light. The stereo pounded Eric Clapton and Led Zeppelin and I talked like crazy, which was unusual for me.

Just as I put my straw to another line, a woman with dark curly hair, who I hadn't noticed sitting right next to me, pulled a gun and screamed, "Freeze, police!" She stood and backed slowly away as a group of pumped-up guys in dark uniforms poured down the basement stairs with more guns. Rousted from the sparkling table, we were handcuffed and shoved into a paddy wagon.

Rob was eighteen, so he went to jail, but I was released pending a hearing. I convinced the police not to call Dad; I lied that he'd beat me. Before court, I met briefly with a public defender who got the charges knocked down to "unlawful gathering" by playing up my clean record and describing me as a small-town girl overwhelmed by big-city life. I pled guilty and promised to stay out of trouble.

But, of course, I didn't. I liked cocaine. It was an adult drug that bestowed adult qualities such as confidence, glamour, and the knack for witty repartee. I appreciated the drug's scarcity and was drawn to its surrounding rituals, the pretty silver and glass accompaniments. I snorted coke whenever I got the chance. I knew who to look for at parties and they knew to look for me. Soon, I augmented my marijuana sales with cocaine sales, just enough to pay for what I inhaled.

Cocaine eyes were difficult to hide from Dad, in part because he'd done plenty himself and recognized the twitchy mannerisms. He must have noticed the changes in me, but he didn't say a word. Nor did he mention the gash in the driver's side door of the Fiat—inflicted when, high on coke, I'd misjudged the placement of a gas pump (a few months later I'd run it into a Buick). I'd done plenty, but I hadn't yet broken the rules we'd tacitly agreed upon. I was still home each morning. I still carved time for pepper-steak dinners and father/daughter banter, allowed him to believe that he was on the inside of my life and I was on the inside of his.

Then, one night, I dropped acid and couldn't drive home. I thought if a friend called and explained my state to Dad, if she offered to gladly see me home in the morning, he'd let it lie. I misjudged. It was after 3 A.M. when the ringing woke my father from the sofa. He said, "No, that's not okay. Put Jennifer on the phone." He told me he was dressing and coming right over. He was no fool. Tight and mad, he ordered me to wait by the curb. The car ride was a test of wills. We didn't speak.

In the living room, I attempted an explanation.

"Dad, I just overdid it a little." My pupils must have been expansive black ink. "It's no big deal."

"Just go down to your room." He pointed forcefully toward the door, commanding me to the dungeon.

"But, Dad!"

"Just go down to your room!" When I didn't budge, he came at me hands first, as if driving for a tackle. He hustled me toward the entryway that led downstairs, swung open the door, and shoved me through. Shocked, I turned to stare at him. That was when he lobbed the insult meant both to conjure images of unsavory behavior and indict my affinity for losers: "You're exactly like your mother!" He slammed the door in my face.

*   *   *

I'd been packing for weeks. I'd boxed the most nonvisible nonessentials first (sweaters, photographs, books), items whose absence Dad wouldn't notice should he come down to use the jean stretcher or iron a shirt. I'd stacked the laden boxes in a shadowy corner behind the waterbed. Items from my room slowly vanished until I was left with my toothbrush and the clothes I was wearing.

Then, one day, after my father left for "work" in his business suit, my friend Anita and her mother arrived. The three of us moved quickly, loading everything into her car. When my bedroom was empty except for the waterbed, the lamp, and the stereo, I perched a note on the coffee table in front of the TV:

Dear Dad,
    I know this is going to come as a surprise, but I've moved out. It's nothing personal. I love you very much and am very glad I came to live with you. It's just that I want to be on my own now. I knew that if I told you, you'd never let me go. Don't bother trying to find me, because I won't come back. And don't worry about me, I can take care of myself.

                                                      Love,
                                                      Jennifer

My destination was a first-floor apartment my boyfriend Crip and I had rented on Fifteenth Street in a crummy section of Minneapolis. It had been difficult to find a landlady willing to rent to us—a jobless teenager and his runaway girlfriend. My father had despised Crip from the beginning. He'd recognized right away the smart, smooth, crooked quality, the smirk behind the smile. Crip was English and looked it: thin, with chocolate brown eyes, a large nose, and gray teeth. He was dangerous, cruelly magnetic.

Crip's reputation was that he hadn't been faithful to any girl. I'd set out to be the first, sharing secrets never before uttered, swearing suicide when we fought. We first had sex in my bedroom in the basement. Dad was asleep and oblivious. I played Molly's *Led Zeppelin II* and we undressed by candle glow. I told Crip I was a virgin and performed a decent impression of one, grimacing at the pain and lying perfectly still (*I am the swan, I am the rose*). I'd wanted the bond between us to be first-time strong.

In the living room of the Fifteenth Street apartment, Anita and I unpacked the boxes I'd so clandestinely filled. We sang to records with the windows open and hung posters and memorabilia. We were discussing my great new life when I glanced outside and spotted Dad's Cadillac at the curb. A chill stole over me. I panicked. My father had never beaten me, it was true, but certainly his temper had been triggered by my sudden departure. Then came pounding on the door.

"Jennifer, are you in there? This is your father! Open the door!"

Instead of opening the door, Anita and I crawled out the apartment's back window and, barefoot and in shorts, dashed away in the spring rain, tramping along downtown streets. When we returned a few hours later, there was a note scribbled in Dad's hand on the kitchen table. Apparently, the landlady had let him in. The note said if I didn't come home immediately, I'd be consigned to a center for delinquents. *You're still only 17, you know!* But the threat was hollow. I knew my father wouldn't go to the police. He mistrusted the law more than I did. I waited a few days and called him from a pay phone. He'd softened. We agreed to have dinner together.

Not long after, Dad parked at the curb again, this time when I wasn't home. Crip, feeling every bit the man of the house, strode into the street. He expected that the two could discuss rationally my quitting high school to move into a broken-down apartment building with a male of dubious prospects. He approached the Cadillac. Just as he made it to the window, my father swung the massive driver's-side door square into Crip's kneecaps. Dad followed up the bruising with some threats—man to man—about taking better care of me, about moving me out of the goddamned ghetto. Then he drove off.

Crip admired my father after that, described him to our friends as a gangster, a truly scary man. I have to admit, I was touched that Dad was willing to fight for me.

14

May 1995

AGENT KAWATERS PHONED to warn me that Dad's case would be featured on an upcoming episode of *Unsolved Mysteries,* the television show hosted by Robert Stack that tantalized with stories of amazing escapes, UFO sightings, and, as it turned out, counterfeiters on the lam. Kawaters's tone was paternal and solicitous, an indication that any reasonable person would have been unnerved by the prospect of her father's criminal life being aired during prime time. All I could think to ask was, "Jesus, couldn't you at least have gotten his story onto a more respectable program, like *America's Most Wanted*?" Kawaters, unfazed, answered that he'd tried, but *America's Most Wanted* was currently in reruns. The episode would air in less than a week, on May 12.

The myriad interviews and "Wanted" posters hadn't yielded much useful information for the marshals. They weren't any closer to catching Dad than they had been on January 23, when he'd disappeared. Kawaters was quoted in a tiny Minnesota newspaper describing my father as an "unpredictable man" whose life had been "spiraling out of control." He admitted that his office was baffled as to Dad's whereabouts. "It's not been going well. We've been interviewing Vogel's relatives and close associates in an attempt to get information. But he was an introvert. He kept to himself a lot. So far, we're not having much luck."

For months, memos had volleyed between Minneapolis and the *Unsolved Mysteries* offices in Burbank, California. The marshals mailed information packets describing Dad's personal preferences ("The subject smokes cigarettes [no particular brand]") and police photos. Kawaters agreed to fly to Los Angeles for three days in order to costar in the segment. In return for an on-camera interview and assistance as a technical consultant, he would receive airfare to L.A., a free hotel room, a complimentary rental car, plus a $40 per diem. *Unsolved Mysteries* submitted script drafts for the marshals' approval. They were critiqued and returned, problems noted, marching orders declared. One memo read, "Again, I would like to reiterate that the other individuals mentioned in the intelligence report—specifically the fugitive's [*blank*]—have not been charged with a crime, and if mentioned, could lead to legal consequences as well as compromise the continuing investigation."

Filming took place all in one day at Grant High School in North Hollywood. Rooms normally utilized for such benign purposes as basketball were recast as dark, underworld settings and backdrops for demonstrations of police efficiency. The custodian's supply closet was transformed into the police evidence room. The school's athletic facility became the outside of Dad's shop. The gardening shed doubled as the storage locker where the police discovered the bulk of his counterfeit money. And the school's front desk served as Speedy Express, the locale in Brownsville from which he'd mailed the fateful package.

Despite the patent silliness of *Unsolved Mysteries,* I was unable to keep the upcoming episode to myself. I told close friends. It was like rolling up my sleeve to show a scar: I courted sympathy and admiration because I'd endured the slip of the knife. The show, I thought, would reveal Dad to be a modern-day John Dillinger, a man more suave and devilish than my cryptic descriptions had suggested. I'd sit back and let Robert Stack do the talking. By the time the credits rolled, my friends would be astounded. We'd share a big laugh.

These were good, decent people, my friends. They worked regular jobs and drank Leinenkugel's beer. Most had attended Hopkins High, my alma mater. Together, we planned canoe trips down the St. Croix. We gathered weekly for motorcycle rides or whiskey and darts. I didn't need to prove a thing. On May 12, Friday night, an hour or so before showtime, I knocked at the door of the house where my friends had gathered, a bottle of Jim Beam and a pound of mini-pretzels in a crumpled paper sack. We kidded around as if nothing important was about to happen. On and around the grimy sofa, we sat in a huddle, next to an enormous coffee table layered with beer cans, card decks, and a smelly, overflowing ashtray. The television was perched at eye height.

By the start of *Unsolved Mysteries,* I was half-drunk and in hysterically high spirits. I laughed uproariously and poked shots at my mostly male friends in a way that prompted Joe, the most blunt of them, to compare me, derisively, to Roseanne Barr.

We hushed and watched and drank. The show's first segment was about the Ouija board and a spirit named Patience Worth who, in the early 1900s, supposedly dictated novels from the other side. This was going to be more embarrassing than I'd anticipated. Dad would be packaged as phenomena; not only that, but his segment would come after the one about the Ouija board. After the Ouija board! We watched in silence as actors in period clothing tried to look mystical behind gauzy lens filters. Then, finally, came the teaser: "Next, join the hunt for a master counterfeiter who printed up millions in bogus bills!"

Stack appeared on camera wearing an impeccably pressed dark suit, his hair blow-dried into a pith helmet. He stood rigidly before an official United States Customs Service seal, a sliver of American flag visible at his left. His face looked vaguely reptilian. Even when he opened his small, tight mouth to speak, his eyes didn't move. They remained cold and dark, boring straight into the camera.

"In January of 1995, an alert shipping clerk in the border town of Brownsville, Texas, tipped off authorities to suspected narcotics activity. Investigators jumped on the lead. They never dreamed that their routine drug case would take a surprising twist and blow the cover of a master counterfeiter who was literally making millions."

The camera zoomed in on Stack's face as he uttered with emphasis, "*literally making millions.*"

The actor chosen to play Dad for the show's hammy reenactments wore a red-and-black plaid jacket that made him look like a Montana deer hunter. His face was all wrong too: he had a long nose, rheumy eyes, and a horrid comb-over. Standing at a counter, passing bills to a woman playing a Speedy Express clerk, he fidgeted and acted suspicious. Never, I thought, would Dad be so obvious, so lacking in charm. To my friends, I jovially threatened to call *Unsolved Mysteries'* 800 number to lodge a complaint.

Clerk: What are you shipping today?
Dad: What do you mean?
Clerk: What's inside the box?
Dad: What . . . well, what did I put down on the form?
Clerk: You wrote down "clothes."
Dad: Yeah, that's right . . . clothes.

The actor hesitated and raised an eyebrow before stammering "clothes." The camera lingered on his face. Eerie music cranked up in the background.

As the segment continued, Stack announced that my father was "no stranger to the law." He recounted a sparse but conspicuous criminal history, while a photograph of Dad wearing a brown polyester shirt filled the screen. It was the same image printed in the newspaper the day I discovered he was gone. His face was supposed to be menacing, but it radiated pain. The eyes, large and in color, appeared as sad and scared as those of a stepped-on dog. I didn't want him to look this bad. My friends, who had never met my father and had very little information with which to counter the pathetic portrait being drawn by *Unsolved Mysteries,* poured more drinks. I stared at Dad's face. Had he earned this level of humiliation? The camera slowly zoomed in on the photo while I sank into the couch.

The return to cartoonish dramatizations was a relief. The show cut to a replica of Dad's shop. The room was filled with blue smoke and illuminated by creepy, atmospheric lighting. "Dad" was standing next to a printing press, brushing away dust with a rag. He wore wire-rimmed glasses ("The subject wears wire-rimmed glasses") and a tan shirt tucked into his pleated trousers. As he dawdled, seven actors dressed like policemen sauntered in. The lead officer wore a bulletproof vest that read "Secret Service" over a white dress shirt and tie. He held his gun loosely, like a spoon at dinnertime. He was absurdly polite.

Lead cop: You John Vogel?
Dad: Yeah.
Lead cop, showing a badge: Federal agents. We have a warrant
    to search your premises.
Second cop, locating the Brownsville box: Got the package!
Lead cop: Mr. Vogel, you're under arrest.

The show's spooky score accented a series of genuine police photographs. First came a close-up of a blue printing press, situated beside a shelf of ink bottles. Next was a desk covered with messy piles of papers and yellow padded envelopes plump with bills. Last was a photo of an envelope torn open, the money fanned out for display. The camera pulled in on the bills, as if honing in on truth itself. These were images of a shop I'd never visited. I scanned for details, secret clues the police would have missed—branded sandwich wrappers, cigarette packs, scrap-paper doodles, pictures on the walls. But there was nothing.

Stack voiceover: Authorities nabbed Vogel just in time. Though he had pressed millions in phony bills, he had circulated less than fifty thousand dollars' worth.

Once again came the pained face, followed by Dad's mug shot front and side, a photo of his car, and, last, the "Wanted" poster.

Stack voiceover: On January 17, 1995, Vogel was released on a personal recognizance bond. He promptly disappeared and has not been seen since. John Bryson Vogel is six-two, one hundred eighty pounds. His brown hair is thinning and turning gray. Vogel has used the aliases J. Johnson, J. Stewart, and Robert Timmers. Vogel is believed to be driving this car, a 1986 Oldsmobile Regency, Minnesota plates 336 CNJ. Authorities consider John Vogel to be armed and dangerous. If you have information, please contact the United States Marshals Service or call our toll-free number, 1-800-876-5353.

I was so outraged I couldn't speak. I grabbed my jacket and keys and fled the house, speeding off in the Escort. My head felt queasy, laden with foul liquid. The images, the words, they wouldn't settle. I couldn't make them settle: the smug portrayal of Dad, the caricature, the wrong impression, packaged according to clumsy, obvious motives. The journalist in me bristled—*This is how the public learns about law, about warrants and drug interdiction?*—but the epicenter quaked somewhere else entirely.

Dad had been portrayed without charm or sophistication, two qualities I counted on in him. I suddenly realized just how much. In recent years, there had been clues suggesting he was no longer the dashing daredevil, but I'd ignored them. As long as he possessed savoir faire, a Continental demeanor, I could separate him from the thugs of the world. And by extension, I could consider myself not the daughter of a graceless cutthroat, but the daughter of a fascinating eccentric—a man to be admired and marveled at, if not trusted and loved up close.

Attributing to him charm and sophistication allowed me to believe he'd chosen his fate. He'd made decisions, terrible decisions, which had justified my own decision to reject him. Considering

Dad in this new light, as desperate and anguished and utterly lost, made him eligible for sympathy. With sympathy came guilt.

I'd walked the most convenient route, the one where Dad was a two-dimensional image, a collection of characteristics in a frame on the wall. By discarding him, his sweet Chap Stick smell, the way he could lift himself perpendicular to any small tree just to impress, I'd mastered the illusion of distance. Now it was coming undone. Jesus, I still loved him. I plopped down on the sofa in my apartment and watched a recording of the show over and over.

Meanwhile, the phones were lighting up at the *Unsolved Mysteries* call-in center in Burbank. On Friday nights, according to promotional materials, the center was staffed by thirty operators standing by to answer calls from the show's approximately 20 million viewers. As the producers had suggested, a U.S. marshal and a Secret Service agent were on hand at the phone center to follow up on hot tips.

The marshals' office in Minnesota was on high alert as well. Updated "investigative packages" had been issued to every district office in the country. Information about Dad had been posted at major U.S.-Mexico border crossings, just in case he tried to break through the tightening law enforcement net, now double-weaved by millions of TV watchers. According to internal memos, agents were scheduled to work extended shifts—from 8:30 A.M. to midnight—on May 12, so they could "field incoming calls and prioritize the probability of the information being timely and accurate." They were instructed to forward relevant names and details and even, if necessary, physically pursue leads themselves. They packed overnight bags so they could leap from their desks and race by plane, train, or automobile to my father's hideout.

The leads were plentiful and varied. A man in Florida was convinced Dad had sold him a mattress at a store called Discount Mattress. Another thought he worked at a Firestone shop in Maryland. A woman in Wyoming said she'd seen my father at a funeral. One in Colorado was certain he lived in her condominium complex. A man in California claimed to have seen a car like Dad's drive into the parking garage of a local hotel. A couple who'd just returned from Las Vegas said my father, working as an MGM Grand cashier, had passed them a counterfeit hundred-dollar bill. There was even a caller who fingered Dad for the Oklahoma City bombing.

None of the tips panned out.

15

At least he didn't shoot anybody

O N A SATURDAY MORNING in July 1985, Dad knocked at the door of the house in Minneapolis I shared with Crip, my friend Jennifer, and an aspirin addict named John. He arrived early, before the heat of the day made it impossible to drink coffee or discuss topics of real importance. I invited him in, offered a cup of General Foods International. My roommate John slouched on the sofa wrapped in Jennifer's pink chenille bathrobe, his brown hair matted, a Marlboro stuck between his lips. With my fingernail, I scraped dried globs of cocktail sauce from a seat cushion and offered Dad a chair.

My father pretended not to be irritated by my living arrangement. He averted his eyes from the cluster of bottles in the corner, the loose wires protruding from the wall, the sweeping splatters of candle wax, our mangy cat La Cucaracha. He crossed his legs and leaned forward on his elbow. When John rose and loped, yawning and scratching his lower back, toward the bathroom, Dad flashed him an unexpected smile.

I sat down on the sofa. "What brings you here so early?"

My father lit a cigarette and waved out the match in a crazy figure 8. "Oh, I don't know. I just thought I'd come over and visit my number-one daughter."

"Dad."

"Okay, you're right. Always getting to the point." He sipped his coffee. "I'm moving to Seattle."

"You're kidding. When did you decide this?" My father and I were equally enamored of chuck-it-all fantasies, and Seattle, with its fog and lush greenery and perch at the edge of the continent, was a favorite dream destination of ours.

"About a week ago, I guess. I don't know what else to do. I've really had it, you know? With everything. With Molly, the little liar. Did you know she was arrested for forging prescriptions? I have no idea what she'll do next. I tell you, Jennifer, only believe about eighty percent of what your heart says. Always keep a little in reserve. As you and I both know, there's always some charming and conniving little fake out there looking to break your heart."

"Yeah, but are you sure moving is the right—"

"Yes."

"Did you and Molly break up?"

"I'm done. Finito. I realize you like Molly, but please don't talk to her. And after I leave, don't tell her where I've gone. Don't tell anybody. Trust me, I'll explain why someday."

I hated it when Dad asked me to stand between him and other people. I thought if anyone inquired, I'd tell the truth. "What's really going on? Are you okay?"

"Sure. Don't worry about me." He mumbled the words sadly into his shirt, begging me to worry.

"How will you survive out there? Do you have money?"

"I've got enough. In fact, I've got enough for two."

"For two?" I knew what he meant.

"I was hoping you'd consider leaving all this behind." He waved his hand, indicating irony. "I was hoping you'd move with me." The implication was that my life was as messed up as his. I would have picked a fight had it not been true.

Dad didn't unveil the storm of catastrophe driving him from Minnesota—exposing the innards of his worry would have meant destroying the one place he could go to escape it—but he was facing plenty. Mom was staging a last stand for child support. Convinced he'd inherited a significant sum from Grandma Margaret, she'd hired an attorney to recoup the estimated $40,000 he owed in back payments. He was also being legally pursued by a number of ex-customers and business partners. They'd filed civil suits totaling upward of $130,000. Then there was the trouble with Molly, who was high most of the time and sleeping with other men. Dad was depressed, even more than usual. Something dark was blotting out a meager sun. I knew that on most nights, he sat by himself in the town house living room, smoking cigarettes and watching television with the shades drawn. The move to Seattle was the best he could come up with, a last chance.

I was eighteen and a high-school dropout. I lived with my friends in a ramshackle one-bedroom house owned by a short, round-headed man whose name actually was Charlie Brown. The windows were so loose in their frames and the walls so devoid of insulation that our shampoo froze solid during the winter. I worked evenings peddling the *Star-Tribune* newspaper over the telephone. I didn't like phone sales, nor was I particularly good at it, but my prospects were limited. I'd walked out on a waitressing job and been canned from a position selling Time-Life Books' Old West series. Several months prior, I'd bussed to the suburbs to apply for a job as a mall clown. I'd arrived early and killed time shoplifting. I was arrested and held in jail for four hours because the police found a leather-bound cocaine kit and friend's ID in my backpack. I guess they thought I might be a drug kingpin on her way to a clown job interview. To cap a generally subpar existence, I'd recently discovered that Crip was sleeping around.

Needless to say, I couldn't think of a single reason to say no to my father. "When would we leave?"

The pleading vanished from Dad's face. He uncrossed his legs and rose from the chair. "I was thinking in a couple of weeks. As soon as possible."

"Okay, I'll go. My answer is yes."

The two of us drove to an all-you-can-eat Chinese buffet and waited in the parking lot for the orange "Open" sign to appear. At the end of our happy conspirators' lunch, after we'd licked our fingers clean of sweet-and-sour sauce and strings of moo goo gai pan, Dad snapped open his fortune cookie. He pretended to read, "Yankee pig, you will die."

By August, we were headed out of Minneapolis on Interstate 394, which connects to I-94, which leads to the West. Dad had sold the Cadillac and purchased a rust-colored, 1977 Chevy station wagon. I was surprised by the trade—the station wagon didn't seem swanky enough—but he assured me with a proud pump of the gas pedal that the car possessed other, perhaps more important, attributes. Why my father needed a 350 engine, I wasn't sure. Apparently he was in a hurry. The distance between Minneapolis and Seattle is almost 1,700 miles, yet Dad insisted that by downing one cup of black coffee per hour, he could burn straight through. Examining road maps and taking measurements against the length of his pinky, he determined that we'd arrive at our destination in less than thirty-five hours, bathroom and meal breaks included.

Lunch and dinner comprised sandwiches and Cokes grabbed from roadside diners in Minnesota and North Dakota; "impersonal chain restaurants," as Dad called them, were out of the question. My father regaled me with topographical and historical facts about each state we passed through. These were the kinds of details he loved—charming details, vacation details. Little Bighorn Battlefield, the Ulm Pishkun buffalo jump, the Continental Divide. We snapped grinning Polaroids of each other standing before billboards and scenic overlooks, and enlisted strangers to photograph the two of us together. In the photos, we appear incongruous, I in my tube top and cutoff jeans and Dad in his dress shirt, loafers, and highway-patrolman sunglasses.

Early the second morning, as the sun rose over the Sapphire Mountains just outside Missoula, Dad reached over and shook me by the shoulder. Our belongings were packed solid to the ceiling and all the way up to the front seat, so there remained little room for sleeping. I'd pulled my knees up to my chest, forming a ball. My head was wedged into the seat crack. Dad turned up the volume on Chopin's Nocturnes. Each piano stroke was like a fingertip against my eyelids.

"Wake up, snickelfritz. You've got to see this."

I squinted through one eye, piratelike, trying to focus. I couldn't believe my father was still behind the wheel, that we were actually in the station wagon barreling toward Seattle. I croaked, "Oh, yeah."

"Tell me that right there isn't the most beautiful thing you've ever seen. I bet you can't." He turned up the music another notch to complement the visuals. The inside of the car was operatic.

The sun blossomed enthusiastically as I unfurled my limbs. I was half-asleep and swaddled in red and orange beams. Just me and Dad. Wheels against empty highway. I was glad I'd come.

We moved into a moderately priced town house in Kirkland, a suburb that sits across Lake Washington from Seattle. The town house perfectly suited Dad's needs. It was clean, generic, and a safe distance from the city's core. It was low maintenance and represented, if not affluence, at least middle-class stability. It was also anonymous enough to serve as a hideout. At forty-two, my father had been flushed of the urge to draw attention to himself, preferring to get by quietly. He furnished the place in much the same way he'd furnished the town house in Hopkins, with earth tones and prefab shelving and television stands. Our bedrooms were across the hall from each other on the second floor. Mine came with a small balcony abutting a grove of cedar trees that sprouted from a blanket of cedar chips. When it rained, I stood outside with my eyes closed and soaked up the nirvana of fragrant pine.

I frequently rode the bus to downtown Seattle, which, in the mid-1980s, was still a romantic place. The streets were slow-paced, full of musicians and little shops selling ginseng ampules you sucked dry through tiny white straws. I got to know the people who made the sidewalks their living rooms and offices: a guitarist who played Zeppelin's "Hey Hey What Can I Do" every time I walked by, an old man who sold burritos out of the back of his truck, a hippie boy named Aaron I charmed into sleeping with me. In my prized green leather poncho, I wandered Waterfront Park by the sound each morning, smoking Chesterfields. (I'd traded Marlboros for the litterproof filterless brand—"You and thousands of old men," my friends chided.)

Sometimes Dad came looking for me, ostensibly because he was worried. He'd complain about my poor judgment, just as he had in Minneapolis: "All I have to do is drive to the worst part of town and that's where I'll always find you." He was just lonely, though. He wanted me to hide with him in the beige fortress, but that was impossible. I was just starting out and his life was closing in. I was on my way up and he was sliding down.

I landed a job soon after arriving in Seattle—a low-paying, part-time job that required only good feet and a healthy skepticism toward the U.S. government. Four evenings per week I canvassed the city's neighborhoods, collecting money for an anti–nuclear weapons lobby called SANE. My father, given his age and income requirements, had more difficulty finding work. I didn't know it then, but he'd borrowed the money that paid our way to Seattle. We'd arrived with $8,500, which was fast running out.

Dad wrote a two-part résumé. The first page expanded, exaggerated, and reconstructed his personal and work histories so they radiated stability and pluck. Three quarters at the University of Minnesota, during which he'd earned Cs, Ds, and Fs, became a full-fledged education at the UM's School of Business Administration. Ventures that had failed were declared resounding successes, with profits doubled and tripled. He even shaved a few years off his

age, listing himself as thirty-nine. Dad had lived the life of a skip-
ping stone; he had the sort of experience you couldn't be honest
about and still land a humdrum job with a respectable company.
He was an entrepreneur, a man of leisure, reduced to begging for
jobs from paunchy, balding human resources managers. On pages
two and three of his résumé, Dad allowed his creativity to burst
through. He listed every skill he possessed (and a few he didn't) in
alphabetical order, starting with "Administration, advertising,
appraising, apartment building owner/mgr, architect, artist, art
supply salesman, antique trader, applicator." He ended with "yacht
captain/builder/owner" and "zoning & planning." Dad tried to
present himself as a Renaissance man, but the list came off as
wacky, an embodiment of his peculiar brand of impractical cleverness. Somehow, he landed a handful of job interviews, but he was
told that he was underqualified, overqualified, or simply too old.

Door-to-door canvassing wasn't bad work. An old, crazy man
pulled a shotgun on me but a young, crazy man declared me a bona
fide angel from heaven. During my rounds one day, I knocked on
the door of a pretty woman in her forties who played violin with the
Seattle orchestra. She was soft-spoken and kind in the same creamy
way Debbie had been. Her house exhibited subtle taste. We talked
for nearly an hour in her living room (at SANE headquarters, I'd
been instructed to resist the spiderlike temptations of lonely people), and she explained that her husband had died years ago. Sadness still clung to her. I talked about my father, with the intent of
fixing them up. A quality woman to soften his rough edges. She
offered two tickets to an upcoming French opera she was playing in.

The seats at the opera were close to the stage, the music gorgeous. However, Dad was fidgety from the start. He whispered dis-
paraging comments about the costumes and quizzed me on current
news events until I finally shushed him. My own father, the classical
music lover. Then he floated a bribe. If we left at intermission, he'd
take me out for Chinese. I acquiesced.

I'd never known him to be nervous about women. I suppose this new attribute was part of his overall disintegration—the backslide in looks, the narrowing of options, the growing remorse. He kept saying, "Nothing I do is ever good enough." It didn't help that he was 1,700 miles from a home he'd stealthily abandoned without good-byes, or that it was always dark in Seattle and raining every goddamned day.

One evening, I returned home to find Dad finishing a painting, acrylic on canvas. He'd always wanted to give brushwork a try, he said. There was an empty vodka bottle on the counter behind him, but he didn't seem drunk. He invited me to inspect his work of art, his masterpiece of crazy boredom. The painting is of a woman who is also a dog. She is reclining nude on a bed amid blue sheets rumpled like the ocean. She has giant round breasts, one of which obscures part of her face and doubles as a dog nose. Her brown hair is divided into high ponytails, which also look like dog ears. She is reaching her hand out, welcoming the viewer into the four-poster bed with her.

I was immediately offended by this depiction of womanhood. "Wow, Dad, that's really screwed up."

"What? Don't you see it? There are two images in one. It's like a double entendre." He was so caught up in this tiny bit of cleverness that he didn't fully realize the message he was trumpeting. It struck me that the painting represented a significant problem: if Dad saw women as dogs—dirty, promiscuous—then maybe it hadn't been people in general who had disappointed him. The painting assigned blame. He'd been tricked, bamboozled, and more than once, it seemed. I reflected on his ability to charm, how the waitresses at Jennings flirted and tried to get him to ask for their numbers. The primary motive behind the spell he cast must have been revenge.

"Who is that supposed to be?" In my head, I took inventory: Mom, Debbie, Molly, me. "It's nobody. I made it up. Come on now. What's the matter? Don't you see it? It's a double entendre!"

Then I realized. Whether or not he knew it, he'd painted his mother, Grandma Margaret.

For Dad's birthday in October, I gave him a supermarket German chocolate cake along with a poem I'd written. I was about to leave for Santa Rosa, California, to stay with Jennifer and her beau. My father hadn't tried to dissuade me from going. Perhaps he was happy to be free of supporting me for a while, relieved that I wouldn't be around to watch him melt down or spin out or whatever he was doing. He'd even handed me a wad of bills for bus fare. Dad blew out the candles on the cake and then opened the envelope containing the poem, which I'd entitled "The Two of Us." It was a horrible piece of writing, clumsy and fraught with atrocious rhymes like, "Through the years, long and wearing, with you my dreams I will be sharing." It pledged undying love and swore eternal loyalty and understanding. By the time he finished reading, he was crying.

I spent the next month in Santa Rosa smoking pot, dropping acid, and eating ice cream in the park. Jennifer and I listened to blues music on Sunday mornings and sipped herbal tea while our hair dried in the sun. I talked to Dad every couple of weeks, though for the most part I'd pushed him from my thoughts. Once, he called just after I'd sucked down the better part of a joint. I was so high that when another call beeped in, I clicked over and talked until I'd forgotten whether I'd said good-bye to my father. I hung up the phone and went for a bike ride.

It was around this time that he purchased a .38 pistol.

I had no plans, except to travel to Iowa for Christmas. It would be my first trip to Mom's house in more than two years. There were good reasons for the pilgrimage: nostalgia for snow, a craving for homemade fudge and peanut brittle. Mostly, though, I missed my mother. She and Doc had finally split up. My indignation over the events of Cedar Rapids had subsided. It was time to patch things over. I invited Dad along so he could join in the merriment and, against my expectations, he accepted. Much as he had with that silly, botched attempt at grafting together family photos, I thought I could repair history. I hoped to foster a cohesive, happy family, if only for Christmas. I thought the idea terribly Zen.

I don't remember much of what happened that Christmas, except that it was uncomfortable. Mom and Dad sat quietly and politely, smoking from separate ashtrays. She offered a spare bed, but he insisted on sleeping on the couch. No need to put anyone out, he said. An attack disguised as courtesy. There's a photo of me and Dad commemorating the holiday. We're sitting side by side with our arms slung around each other on Mom's flowered sofa next to a wooden nativity scene. Glasses of champagne rest on the table with a pack of Carltons. I've got bushy long hair and a clear, smiling face. Dad looks tired. His eyes are puffy and encircled by bruise-brown shading. He's grinning, but he looks as though he's been crying for forty years.

My father flew back to Seattle a month before I did. I drove to Minneapolis, in order to spend time with Anita, who was engaged to a hot-tempered Harley rider. I was standing in her kitchen when Dad called. It was late January. He sounded in the dumps.

"Dad, I'm flying in on February eleventh. Can you pick me up at the airport?"

"Well, actually, I might not be home. I'm going out of town on business. Could you have a friend meet you?"

"Sure. But what kind of business? Did you get a job?"

"We'll see. The prospects look good. Got a line on one anyway. Honey, the reason I called is to say that if anything should happen to me, I love you. You're my swan. Remember that."

"What do you mean? You aren't going to hurt yourself, are you?"

"No, of course not." He tried to laugh. "You just never know. I could get hit by a bus."

"Do you want me to come home now? I could probably get a flight tomorrow."

"Don't worry. I'll see you in two weeks. Everything's fine."

"You don't sound fine."

He tried the laugh again. "I'm great."

"Okay, but if you get too lonely or something, please call. Dad?"

"Yes."

"Don't do anything drastic."

"Sure, honey. Don't worry. Have fun."

Anita broke things off with the biker and she flew with me to Seattle. I'd arranged for a friend from SANE to pick us up at the airport. The three of us sat around the town house drinking wine until it was time for bed. My father wasn't home, just like he'd said.

Early next morning, I was awakened by a phone call from a cop in Spokane. "I've got some good news and I've got some bad news," he said. "The good news is that your father is okay. The bad news is that he's been arrested for bank robbery." The man rattled off some details: Dad had robbed two banks in Spokane the day before; he'd been captured after a high-speed chase. Caught on the first part of his monologue, I slammed the phone down and sobbed, then ran around in circles, bleary-eyed and screaming, "Business trip, my ass! You son of a bitch!" I rummaged through Dad's closet and observed that he'd packed two suits, an alarm clock, and his briefcase—all for my benefit. On top of the television in his room was a newspaper clipping, a classified ad for a secondhand store that purchased furniture. This was for me as well, a tool with which to tidy up.

I tore the ad to shreds. Was I supposed to be thankful for this lame, booby-prize effort? It felt manipulative. My father wanted me to believe that even in his darkest hour, he'd thought of me.

Later that same day—which I have come to think of as the day of a thousand eternities—a letter from Dad arrived in the mail: *Dear Jennifer, if you're reading this, I've made my bed and have to lie in it.* He wrote that he couldn't reveal where he'd gone (*Just tell people I've moved to Hawaii, okay, honey?*), but that he'd left $3,000, three gold coins, and a key under the carpet in my bedroom. The letter prompted me to sell the furniture and gather the security deposit from our landlady. It also explained that if I took the key from under the rug to a post office box in downtown Kirkland, I'd find a package. The next day, I slid the key into the keyhole and there it was. He'd mailed me a hunk of the robbery money, nearly $4,000 in a fat manila envelope. The writing on the package was a frantic mess. I stood there wondering why he hadn't addressed it before robbing the bank.

The police insisted that I travel to Spokane for an interview. I purchased two bus tickets and Anita and I made the long trek, both of us miserable. Our only comfort was a nice bag of pot, which, by some cruel turn, was stolen during a bathroom break in a bumfuck town in eastern Washington.

The police officer was smug. He told me, with apparent relish, that Dad had admitted to robbing a total of four banks, all the while wielding the .38. Besides the two in Spokane on February 10, he'd robbed a bank in Kirkland on December 12 and another in Eugene, Oregon, on January 30, making off with just over $2,000 each time. The first must have been for Christmas presents. The second took place the day after he'd called me at Anita's. Dad claimed to have spent the money on rent and food, the officer said, but had I noticed any lavish behavior? Did I think he'd robbed more banks? Did I know where any of the money had gone? No, no, and *N.O.* I didn't mention the envelope or the cash from under the rug.

I inquired about the circumstances surrounding the arrest. The officer told me that the first robbery, of Spokane's Great Western Savings Bank, had taken place at 2 P.M. The holdup netted $3,885, none of which had been recovered. He said my father went from the bank to a bar in town, where he drank vodka. Three hours later, he screwed up the nerve to rob a second branch of the same bank. This time, he ordered tellers to open the vault and turn over only large bills; he made off with $27,027. Witnesses described Dad, who wore a wig and sunglasses during the holdups, as "methodical and in control of himself" while leveling instructions to move quickly and do exactly as he said. He'd flashed the .38 but hadn't fired.

Well, that was something. He didn't shoot anybody.

Local cops spotted Dad's station wagon pulling away from the second bank and chased him across town, onto Interstate 90 heading west toward Seattle. Joined by the Washington State Patrol and the FBI, they followed him for nearly an hour at speeds exceeding 100 miles per hour. The 350 engine. A couple of semi drivers turned their rigs to block the road, but Dad swerved into the ditch and around them. The chase finally ended when an officer pumped shotgun fire into one of the station wagon's rear tires. By that time, the car had been riddled with bullet holes. After the police flushed my father from the car at gunpoint, they recovered the money from the second robbery and found a bouquet of flowers with a card for me. The interviewing officer considered the flower purchase absurd, but I understood. Dad had bought them as a superstitious measure—a connection to home that would ensure his arrival there. Now the flowers and card were in a trash bin somewhere.

The officer led me to a holding cell where I could talk with Dad. I sat in a chair and waited, wondering what I would say. Wearing an official-issue jumper, he entered the room, staring at the floor and looking ashamed. *How dare he feel shame!* I took the robberies personally: the way I figured, he'd traded me for money. I didn't care that he'd been faced with the worst financial crises of his life or that all those lonely nights with the bottle had clouded his judgment. My only concern was that he'd abandoned me. Money wasn't worth walking across the street for. It certainly wasn't worth robbing a bank for. He'd thrown everything away: his life, our life.

When he finally made eye contact, I noticed a long, thin abrasion across his forehead. The mark was from where he'd glued on the wig.

"I'm so sorry, honey."

"What's that on your forehead?" I was being cruel.

"Um. I cut myself."

"You can't even tell me the truth now, with everything so obvious."

"If I could take all this back I would. Believe me, all I want is to step back ten years to when you were a little girl and everything was going so well."

"Well, you can't."

"No, I guess I can't."

I couldn't wait to get away.

Soon after I returned to Seattle, Dad's public defender called to say he knew about the package. He promised that if I gave back the money, the court would show leniency toward my father. I hadn't settled on keeping it anyway, representative as it was of skewed priorities and desertion. I turned it over.

I kept the bills and gold coins from under the rug, however. For weeks, Anita and I lived the high life—we bought and ate and traveled in the aggressive manner of desperate, angry people. Then, at last, I began addressing practical matters. I called the landlady, who informed me that the rent hadn't been paid in months and no deposit would be forthcoming. I called the used-furniture store, which bought all our major pieces for around $200. Then I sorted through my father's personal belongings, organizing everything into two stacks: One comprised sentimental items that would be shipped for safekeeping to Anita's house in Minneapolis. The other included disposable possessions that would be thrown out or given away. I cycloned through each room, reserving Dad's bedroom for last.

I stripped his bed and folded the brown sheets into neat squares (I'd keep and use them for fifteen years after). I emptied the nightstand drawers, where I found socks, various business cards, and an old, empty pot pipe. I removed the few pictures Dad had propped about the room, opening the backs to check for hidden money. Then I started on the closet. I organized his clothes inside a suitcase, to be shipped and saved for when he was again a free man. The painting of the woman-cum-dog, which was propped behind a small shoe collection, I wrapped for shipping as well. I stood on my toes and, at the back of a high shelf, spied a traveling salesman's rectangular briefcase. I set it on the bed and popped the latches. Inside was a trove of letters and school papers from when Nick, Liz, and I were kids. He'd kept everything: Christmas lists, report cards, name tags from our cribs in the hospitals where we'd been born. There was a thick stack of photographs too: the cabin on Round Lake, the baby ducks, Dad sanding wood atop the *Razzmatazz,* Debbie in a New Orleans cafe holding a cigarette. Wrapped in a T-shirt was a framed portrait we'd had taken a decade earlier at a shop in Brainerd. Nick, Liz, Dad, and I wear Wild West costumes and stoic, sepia-toned faces.

I ran my hand through my hair and marveled at how a man could be so good and so bad at the same time.

Anita and I mailed eighteen boxes to Minneapolis. Everything else we gave away our last night in the town house. It was nearing midnight, the deadline for evacuation, when I began knocking on doors, searching for someone who'd welcome a load of miscellany. I found a fresh divorcée, living alone with her young son. She and her boy relay-raced from our town house to hers with pillowcases of ketchup, crackers, magazines, towels, and dishes. When she asked if there was anything she could do for us, we requested a bottle of whiskey. She brought us one.

We pulled the door shut and slipped away. With our belongings bundled in luggage soon to be ditched for backpacks, Anita and I ran to catch the last ferry to Bainbridge Island. The future lay wide and open.

16

I got to thinking

D AD CONFESSED TO THE four bank robberies
after securing a plea agreement by which he'd be
charged with only one. He viewed the admissions as a show of good
faith, a method of clearing his conscience with no tangible conse-
quence. While unburdening himself, he took the opportunity to
explain to the court the circumstances preceding the robberies.
Surely, he thought, the events of the past four years justified his
actions. The court would see that. It would take pity on him.

He spilled it all, the long spiral downward, which, by his estimation, began in 1982 after Debbie left, tired of waiting for a marriage
proposal. He talked of business failures, declining markets, lawsuits,
his mother's sudden heart attack in 1983, Molly and the forged drug
prescriptions, her cheating, and me—my running away from Mom's
house in Cedar Rapids and foisting upon him the position of caretaker, a role for which he was ill prepared. He said he'd begun drinking in earnest at the sight of Debbie's back, and the more bleak
things had become, the more he'd drunk. Consequently, the more
bleak things had become. Toward the end, he'd polished off a fifth of
vodka a day.

He described for the court our move to Seattle, how he planned
it in the hopeful yet defeated manner of all fresh starts, and how
that effort turned sour when he failed to find work. He ran out of

money—his assets at the time of arrest, he claimed, totaled less than $100, while his debts exceeded $150,000. According to the efficiently worded official summary of Dad's account: "He states his thinking was affected. He drank too much. He then decided to rob a bank." Dad chose the banks in Spokane because he suspected he might get caught and hoped to keep the details off the Seattle TV news. To muster daring before these doomed robberies, he drank. He barely recalled the details.

Judge Alan McDonald condemned my father to fifteen years in prison. Congeniality, he was told, would earn him "good time" and an earlier release. McDonald also levied a special assessment of $50, which Dad would have to work off via dime-an-hour jobs during his incarceration—apparently this was so he might experience the satisfaction of earning his way out of prison and so he wouldn't mistake maximum security lockup for an excuse to be lazy. McDonald did exhibit a little mercy by recommending placement at the federal prison in Sandstone, Minnesota. Dad's public defender had suggested the facility for its proximity to family, "particularly his children, which should reinforce rehabilitation and life without crime."

My father wasn't sent to Sandstone, however, and there wasn't a damn thing he could do about it. The Federal Bureau of Prisons was in charge of such determinations and they'd determined that because he'd wielded a loaded .38 during the holdups, Dad was too high-risk for Sandstone. For months, he rotated among interim jails and prisons until finally, on July 9, 1986, he was shipped to the federal correctional institution in Phoenix, Arizona, a state more like hell than like Minnesota.

During these transfers and negotiations, while his fate was sorted and debated, Dad wrote letters I didn't receive. I was never in one place long enough. Nor did I leave forwarding addresses. My abiding concern was not what might happen to him, but what might happen to me. I'd fled Seattle in need of adventure and revelation. My true character, I hoped, was inside somewhere, buried under generations of familial strife. Into the wild blue yonder I set off, bandanna on stick, the money from under the rug tucked beneath a flap of folded fabric.

Anita and I caught the ferry to Bainbridge and for a few days holed up in a vine-covered farmhouse with two young men. Then, believing the lyrics from that Zeppelin song, we hopped a plane to California. In late February, we touched down in San Jose. We purchased wool blankets at an army surplus store and cut holes big enough for our heads to stick through. We put our thumbs out and hitchhiked south, through Monterey, toward Big Sur, a remote, jagged strip of Pacific coastline mythical in appeal.

As a team, Anita and I worked well. Still reeling from the bank robberies, I acted sort of stunned and inappropriate, either saying nothing or blurting forced profundities. Anita, on the other hand, knew exactly how to talk to people—what to ask and how to ask it. Thanks to her, we never starved or stepped into anything too dangerous. In return for playing ambassador, she required my flat-out loyalty and respect. She didn't make a big deal of it. Nights, we slept side by side in city and state parks, wearing every stitch of clothing we owned for warmth, my blanket on the bottom, hers on top.

It was raining the morning we arrived in Big Sur. Heavy webs of fog clung to the tops of towering redwoods. The Santa Lucia Mountains leaned against one another like sisters. It was quiet, unbelievably quiet, as though Highway 1 had been sealed at both ends. There were no tourists to speak of, just this weird little community living among a handful of shops and lodges; traveling kids, gray-bearded hippies, artists, acid casualties, New Age fanatics, Deadheads, and people who simply wished to be left alone. There seemed to be no eccentricity shunned by the good people of Big Sur. Locals wore buttons that read, "It's only a movie."

Anita and I camped among the redwoods, beneath craggy root structures that protected us from so-called widow makers, the mammoth branches that crack and tumble from on high. Our friend Jennifer came north to join us. It was a perfect setup, the three of us living together in this lost, glorious place. We bathed in icy rivers, picked jade from the hills, and lounged in the California sun, munching avocados with San Luis sourdough. Jennifer and Anita took part-time jobs at the River Inn; I still had Dad's money. We were issued Big Sur residence cards, which afforded us discounts at local businesses. In the early-morning hours, while the guests were asleep, we locals were allowed into the hot springs at Esalen. We soaked atop the cliffs as salt water rushed and crashed below. White on the rocks.

I smoked pot with breakfast each morning. I read Edgar Allan Poe and David Ignatow and wondered what really mattered. Jotting a million notes in my journal, I engaged in tricks of perspective ("The moon looks like the end of a straw, someone is drinking in the night"), paranoia ("Ronald Reagan doesn't look like one of us"), and morbidity ("Death travels disguised as life, erasing the faces of its victims"). I once spent an entire afternoon copying down the good parts of a book called *Legal Highs,* entries that mentioned "tranquillity" or "feelings of well-being." For the most part, I was enjoying myself.

The problem was, I never could fully commit to doing nothing, to being permanently weird or lost or eccentric. There was a voice in my head that said, These people are hiding from something, their rules are flimsy, the center can't hold. If a girl borrowed my sweater, I expected it back, a view considered old-fashioned and sad. One night, asleep on a hill, I dreamed of flying. I was delighted to find myself soaring over bustling sidewalks. I swooped sparrowlike, playfully crinkling my nose at the sun. Then I spotted an ice cream cart and immediately came in for a landing. Even in dreams I was earthbound.

The realm of beauty eluded me. Perhaps I was wicked. I met men named T-bone and Sunshine, but nobody stuck. They couldn't love me, because I couldn't love them. I began to fear that I'd be an outsider my whole life, just like Dad—looking in, wishing. When I complained to Anita that I'd never find "the one," she said, "For

God's sake, you're nineteen. Don't worry about it. You have plenty of time." When I explained that I should never bear children, that my mutant genes should die with me, she looked genuinely shocked. "That's ridiculous. You're no worse than anyone else."

In April, details of the Chernobyl nuclear disaster made their way to Big Sur. There had been an explosion, a fireball that blew apart the reactor's heavy steel-and-concrete lid. I read that thirty people had been killed; 135,000 evacuated due to high levels of radiation. It was the worst such disaster ever. I considered radiation and air currents. Did I detect unusual stomach pains? Was that a budding rash on my hand? I warned the people around me, drawing colorful posters and even writing storyboards for a TV commercial. Mostly, though, my fellow travelers were content getting stoned and watching Bruce Lee movies. The enchantment of Big Sur—the mountains, the sand, the trees—seemed deceptive, lulling. Calming us for the slaughter.

The sense that I should do something about a world gone awry rose slowly and steadily, like a seedling of moral responsibility. I searched everywhere for a hideout, a place to tuck myself away from undue concern: Santa Rosa, Oakland, Monterey, Los Osos, San Luis Obispo, the Chatsworth hills outside L.A., San Diego, Cochise Stronghold in Arizona, Tombstone, down Mexico's mainland and up the Baja peninsula in a VW bus covered with polka dots. All this restless tramping and I still didn't know what I had to offer or whether the future held more than bank robbery and fortune telling.

In early June, I was sitting alone on the edge of a cliff under the wind-formed eucalyptus trees lining Davenport Beach, California, also known as "John's woods." I'd been awake for two days. I saw faces in the branches and leaves. Gazing down at the swirling water and jagged rocks, I realized I could slip off the edge, be pulverized into the sand, and nobody would know. It would be weeks, maybe months, before my family asked after me. I glowered up the coastline at a small but relentless factory chugging smoke beside the ocean. I wanted to blow it up with a bomb. I'd strap dynamite to my body and go out in a blaze of righteousness. I stood, grabbed my backpack, and walked to the nearest pay phone. My brother, Nick, answered. He sounded warm and offered all the right advice. "Why don't you come home?" he said. Mom wired bus fare.

On my last night in California, I smoked heroin at the Motel Continental in Santa Cruz with a quartet of grimy road people. I had poison oak and was covered with calamine lotion. One guy kept pulling open the curtains and jerking his head left and right, paranoid. A girl retched into the toilet. I lay on the bed, floating amid pillows as soft as cotton balls. I smiled quietly, reveling in the white calm, the total absence of stress. I thought this must be how normal people feel.

Early next morning, I folded my clothes into my backpack and tiptoed across strewn bodies toward the door. A boy with dark curly hair lifted his head. "Wow," he whispered. "I can't believe you're actually going back. It takes real guts to leave all this."

I boarded a Greyhound to Iowa via Salt Lake City, a sheet of blotter acid pressed between the pages of my journal. I'd sell the acid to pay Mom back and then I'd get started in Minneapolis. I intended to make new friends and attend college. I would do good, meaningful work and knit myself so thoroughly into other people's lives that my absence for even a single day would cause dismay.

17

The letters were signed with love

June 25, 1986

Dear Jennifer,

It appears I missed you again. I called Liz in Iowa and she said you had left the day before. I also sent a letter to that Oakland address but I guess you'd already left there too. You're just like a phantom—there one day and gone the next!

I'm still in Oklahoma, but will be going to Phoenix next week for sure. I'm going to need some money for shoes and misc. items and Liz's dentist and I won't be working for another month or so. Could you send me $150.00? Do you have enough left to handle that?

Please write and let me know what you've been doing and how you are. I'll write you a LONG letter as soon as I arrive. I won't mention this again (after this last time), but be sure and don't say anything to anybody and please don't contact Molly. I know I asked you before and it didn't do any good. Trust me, I'll explain why someday. If anyone finds out about this I won't be able to move back to Minnesota. Then I'll really be homeless. If anyone asks, tell them I'm living in Phoenix.

Again, I'm sorry to have left you in the lurches and for the embarrassment I've caused.

Love U,
Dad

The letter found me in Minneapolis, where I was living with Anita's mother. It was a relief to learn Dad was all right, that there was an actual address in Arizona. Just as he requested, I didn't mention the robberies or show the letter to anyone. Not even to Anita's mom, who had generously wrapped me in her life of evening dinners and flourishing gardens. She said I could stay in her spare bedroom for as long as I wanted. However, I'd already concocted a formula for imminent liberation.

Step one: Find a job.
Step two: Rent an apartment.
Step three: Start college.

July 16, 1986

Dear Jennifer,

I was *so* happy to get your letter, but at the same time it made me a little sad because it made me miss you even more. Wish I was there right now to give you a big hug. Wish I was there to help you out with an apartment too. I feel as if I left you stranded. Sorry.

Thanks for the money, honey. It'll come in handy 'cause I need tennis shoes and toiletries and misc. items, and this place only pays $.11 an hour. That works out to around $17.00 a month! It doesn't sound like much, but remember, it's tax free.

Phoenix is brand new and not too bad; it's set up like a condominium complex and even has a little shopping "mall" with a dining room, laundry, barber shop, hobby shop, recreation hall, commissary (store), library and chapel. No kidding, each facility has its own door and as you walk under the canopy you feel like you're in a shopping center—like Miracle Mile, maybe.

The priest here is from St. Paul and he's trying to re-convert me and wants me to serve mass. I shouldn't have told him about my altar boy days I guess.

I'm still trying to get home and will have a "team" meeting in about a month. I'll find out then if I can get a transfer to Sandstone or someplace else in the area.

Enough about me—

Are you O.K.? Is everything going to work out for you? I hope you saved some money babe, as I told you in the Oakland letter (which I guess you didn't get), there probably won't be much money coming in July so you'll have to tough it out until December at which time you'll have enough for tuition and living expenses.

I'm glad you decided to live in Minneapolis, it's a nice place to be from and it always seems comfortable. Maybe that's just my feeling. Or, maybe there is something to the "roots" theory. Anyway, I'll be back there eventually.

You sounded a little melancholy in your letter. You're wondering what the future has in store for you and where you're going and what's life all about and so on . . . I wish more than anything, right now, you and I could get all dressed up and go out to dinner and have a long talk.

Just don't worry about anything and don't worry about me. If you have any questions or problems honey, you know you can (I was going to say "come to me") confide in me, by letter of course—for now.

Take care of yourself and be careful. And write.

Love you very much,

Dad

P.S. Will you keep in touch with Nick & Liz?

August 3, 1986

Dear Jennifer,

Things are just great out here in the desert; another hot day—115 degrees in the shade! That's if you can find any shade, elsewhere it's a lot hotter. I can't imagine it being too much hotter, at least not on earth and when a person is alive. Can't imagine either, anyone settling here, the pioneers must have discovered Arizona in the winter.

The only thing happening here is my new glasses. That's right, after all these years of squinting, I'm finally getting specs. Old age is creeping up fast.

Thanks for sending that money, or did I thank you in my last letter? It sounds like you haven't any left of what I gave you in Washington. Can you get by? Can you make it until January? Geez, I worry about you honey. I know I never give you enough credit when it comes to self-sufficiency and you've gotten by before so I suppose you'll just sail along smoothly, right? You can always call Cheryl or your Mother in case of emergency.

Oh, before I forget there was something that happened here the other day. The world's oldest and largest cactus fell over and died. Or the other way around—died and then fell over. It was 78 feet high! That's as tall as an 8-story building. Amazing, huh?

Write if you get a chance.

I love you,
Dad

P.S. Thank you for saving my tapes; I had thought that you dumped all my stuff.

I held no illusions about Dad's ability to support me. I considered his promises of a check in December or January merely the death throes of fatherhood. He was playing a role—one that kept him involved in my life and at the same time alleviated his guilt—from a concrete cell with an exposed toilet some 1,800 miles away. I was on my own. That I knew for certain.

I picked through the guts of my backpack and noticed for the first time, perhaps due to the spare room's clean lace curtains and neat bedspread, that all my shirts were dingy and stained. The cuffs were uniformly charcoal colored. I'd lived for so long on the street that I was becoming the street. Most of my pants had drawstrings or holes in the knees and wouldn't suffice for job interviews. From Anita's pristinely stored wardrobe, I chose a blue flowered skirt and yellow blouse. I hunched over the Sunday want ads and circled job descriptions that interested me. No phone sales. No product surveys. No data entry. I phoned the Minneapolis Police Department to ensure that on my eighteenth birthday my record had been expunged. Within a month, I landed two positions: one as a clerk at a downtown art supply store and another selling concessions at an independent movie house called the Uptown Theatre.

Finding an apartment proved more difficult. My aberrant rental history haunted me. I'd moved from one dwelling in the middle of the night still owing three months back rent and, just to spite the landlady, I'd left behind an overflowing litter box, dirty dishes, and a package of rotting beef. Besides, how could I explain where I'd been for the past year? My life since August 1985 registered as a gap—untrackable and suspicious. I decided that roommates were my best option. Individuals would certainly be more forgiving than management companies with their databases. I answered an ad placed by two young women, a makeup clerk at a department store and a lay liturgist with the Catholic Church. They liked me, as did their German shepherd. I moved in.

August 27, 1986

Dear #1 Daughter,

I just read your letter again and I think you are the most special, most sensitive and the sweetest person I know. I love you a lot.

I also empathize with you in your loneliness. I know how that can be. I know too even when you're with a person, you can still be lonely. As I said, you're very special; if you don't know that by now you must have at least an inkling of it. You are going to meet that special person someday but it may take a long time to find him, and it probably won't be in the circle of friends you have now. It may take 10 years or more (oh, my God, no!).

If I hadn't gotten married at 19, I'm not sure if even I would be now; I don't think I ever found my "soul-mate" (corny but apt term). I guess maybe Debbie came closest, but then again I didn't want to get married, so maybe not. I think everybody hopes for that special person but gives up and settles for 2nd best or 3rd or 4th even, just to have somebody —anybody.

I've been telling you since you were a little squirt that you were a swan among geese; a rose among wildflowers. I think you'll start to realize that from now on. I'm proud of you, the way you're handling yourself—you seem to have matured and grown wiser since Seattle.

It was such a good feeling to get that letter from you— when a few weeks go by and I don't hear anything I automatically figure you don't care and have forgotten me (paranoid, I guess). I wouldn't blame you if you disowned me, I mean because of the situation and this place and all. You don't have to write any more often or anything like that. I'm just trying to tell you that I think about you all the time and am relieved when I learn you are all right and that you still love me.

I went before the "team" on the 13th and didn't find out too much. I will get a transfer to Sandstone *for sure* but don't know when—sometime between now and February. I really need to get back to Minnesota, I feel comfortable there; don't know why, maybe it's roots.

I bought a little walkman stereo radio with earphones. It's so nice to lay back and shut out the world and this place and listen to soft music. Right now they're playing Mozart's "Elvira Madigan." I can escape from this place every night.

Speaking of music, I'm writing a book. "The Composer"(?) is about a book-store clerk who loves classical music and hates rock (no similarities to yours truly). Anyhow, in discussing music with a friend, he opines that anyone with even half a brain could compose and record a rock tune. He then makes a bet that he can do it himself. Later, finding it wasn't so easy and wondering why, "because it all sounds the same, even played backwards" . . . Backwards—that's it. He modifies an old portable record player to play backwards. He then plays (backwards) his entire collection, the top 40, and the 6–8,000 albums carried in the book store.

He finds that about 1 in 12 "new" melodies is actually decent to listen to. Instant success—he sells songs to rock groups, scores movies, "composes" symphonies, etc. etc. and becomes famous and unbelievably rich. Anyhow, it goes on and on and in the end he is asked to run for president. Pretty far-fetched, but it is very much a parody and written completely tongue-in-cheek. I don't know if the premise is novel or if it's been used before. Have you ever heard of an idea like that? If so, let me know, if not, keep it under your hat.

Actually, when you think about it, you probably could "write" a few songs that way.

It's bed time honey, gotta go.

I love you x 100 = Your Dad

At the art store, I worked with a heavyset punk girl who dressed all in black and wore elaborate, antiestablishment purple makeup. She rolled her ebony eyes at our manager and answered questions in a monotone grumble, sometimes slipping me a sly smile. Together, we danced at First Avenue on Tuesday nights and listened to records at her apartment—Prince, Big Black, The Cure, Throwing Muses. We smoked pot and gorged on ice cream straight from the carton. To commemorate our friendship, she presented me with a mixed tape she'd entitled, "I feel more fulfilled making Xmas cards with the mentally ill."

I closed the tape into my Walkman and ambled down Lyndale Avenue at dusk, watching traffic and people inside their homes and offices. This was my favorite way to view the world: separate, yet somehow more acutely involved than if I were inundated with street sounds. In the middle of The Cure's "Hanging Garden," there was a crash. I approached the scene on foot, somehow unable to change course. I neither slowed nor sped up my pace. A man clad in leather, a Harley rider, was lying in the middle of the street, his leg twisted back, blood streaming down his bearded face. Sobbing, he was trying futilely to crawl to the curb. I walked past.

It bothered me, my response to the crash.

About a month later, a friend called. She'd found six tiny, abandoned kittens in a parking garage. Her landlord enforced a no-pet rule, so I adopted them. My mother had ably nursed to health countless birds, cats, and squirrels; surely I was capable of the same. I thought of Mom—her nurse's hands, her concerned mouth—as I constructed a bed of cardboard lined with a fuzzy towel and placed a bowl of warm milk on the floor. The kittens refused to sleep in the bed, nor would they drink the milk. Too young to be separated from their mother, they stood shaking, coated with sticky fur, blind. They kept shimmying under the refrigerator to cuddle the warmth of its motor. Over and over, I scooped them out and forced milk between their strawberry-seed teeth. The kittens died in twos.

The ground was frozen solid, so I placed the kittens in individual plastic bags and buried them in the snow out back, thinking I'd make a proper grave come spring. But the German shepherd dug them up and delivered them, half-eaten, to the doorstep.

November 10, 1986

Dear Number One Daughter,

I'm just sitting around here waiting for my clothes to get done. Exciting, huh? There are only 2 washers and 2 dryers for 240 men and it's an ordeal every week to get to the damn machines. Usually you have to wait in line and spend 3–4 hours per load.

It's getting very crowded here; everybody and everything has been doubled up. I'm glad I've only got a few months left in this place, nice as it is. Incidentally, I talked to my case mgr. yesterday and he said he'll put me in for transfer to Sandstone the end of Dec. or first of Jan. So add another 6–8 weeks for paperwork & travel time and I should get there just as the last snow drift is melting—me and the robins arriving from the south at the same time.

Have you talked to Liz and Nick lately? I haven't gotten a letter from Liz for a while, wonder why . . . I get the feeling some of my letters don't get through—both to you and Liz. Paranoia, I guess. I had asked Liz to send me a Reader's Digest because I need some info out of it to send in a short story I wrote, but never got it. Do you suppose you could send one? Any old Reader's Digest will do.

You know, I've never been anywhere in my life where there weren't damned Reader's Digests all over the place—hundreds of them on shelves, tables, magazine racks, drawers, tops of refrigerators . . . not here. They don't exist in this place.

You mentioned in your letter you liked to talk to strangers. Be careful who you talk to. Do you remember that girl who was stabbed to death over on 30th & Irving? The police know who the guy is and where he lives (Henn-Lake area) but can't prove it.

I'm not trying to scare you honey, just keep that fact in the back of your mind. Back of your sub-conscious would even be O.K. There are so many creeps lurking around out there and you can't tell by appearances or demeanor who they are. You probably get tired of me worrying about you all the time. I guess you can take care of yourself.

By the way, I was real sorry to hear about your cats; a real *cat*astrophe I'd say.

Well, sweetie, I've got to get back to work. Write when you get the chance.

I miss you.

Love, Dad

In Dad's baby book there's an entry written in Grandma Margaret's hand that says, "Jon always liked to be outside." This was the abiding theme of his life. He liked to be outside. Not just sailing the Gulf of Mexico or walking among a patch of Midwestern woods or reclining by a lake at dusk in cutoff shorts, smoking a cigarette. Dad liked to be *outside*. Outside marriage, outside family, outside the dreary nine-to-five business world, outside boredom, outside his head. He pirouetted around people and their problems as if repelled by reverse polarity. In this manner, he attempted to minimize regret and maximize distraction, an elaborate scheme to foil the spider waiting in the hole.

Prisons are, in every sense, inside. Dense concrete walls, pitted and thickly painted with institutional colors; metal doors, fortresslike; tiny windows, veined with wiring. Days are built of routine and utter lack of choice—lights on, head count, line up for breakfast, work, line up for lunch, work, line up for dinner, head count, lights out, lights on. You can't stand in the shadows or disappear even for an hour. There's nothing to do except track seasonal changes and stare at your release date with anticipation and dread. And, of course, pick through the mess that is your life.

The world proceeds without you. Family turns away. You write letters, pretending not to notice, and then add, parenthetically, that you do.

Dad worked hard at his job in Phoenix's graphics department, eyeing that "good time," the dangled early release date. He received stellar evaluations from supervisors, who described him as a conscientious self-starter with "an exceptional learning ability." When he wasn't working, he was pounding away at the stolid federal bureaucracy, attempting to finagle a transfer to Sandstone, eighty miles from Minneapolis. He wrote to staff at the Bureau of Prisons, appealing to their sympathies.

In one letter, he played up his concern for Nick and Liz, reasoning that they needed his support due to a neglectful, alcoholic mother. "If I were in the area," he wrote, "I would worry less and somehow feel more available to them if they had problems. It would also enable me to see them regularly which is very important right now—they're not especially proud of me."

Officially, prisoners are worth very little and their sob stories even less. The bureau declined Dad a transfer to Sandstone, again citing security concerns. They did, however, agree to send him to the federal correctional institution in Oxford, Wisconsin, which, at least, was in the right part of the country.

He arrived in Oxford on March 24, 1987, and succumbed to the usual orientation processes and physical and psychological testing. Doctors reported him to be in good health, while noting traits like "Seems to take no pleasure in anything," "Inattentive; seems preoccupied," and "Gets along with hoods." My father, finally within range of Minneapolis, placed four people on his visitors list—me, Liz, Nick, and Cheryl—and waited for the smiling, familiar faces to arrive.

The mail brought a form I was to complete in order to be cleared for visitation privileges. I provided my name, date of birth, and social security number so the prison could check my background, including any criminal record, and determine whether a visit from me would present a management problem. I signed and mailed the form.

Weeks passed, however, and still I made no plans to go. I let myself think it was a matter of logistics—I didn't have a car or much money. To these technicalities I added the notion that I simply couldn't bear to view my father caged, wearing the cuffs and jumpsuit, leaning forward on the plastic prison chair (that's what I'd later tell Dad, and even his flattened tone when he claimed to "understand completely" wouldn't shake my logic). These were valid excuses, after all. Reasonable responses to circumstances. I'd cling to them, but they were not the real reasons for my absence at Oxford.

I flat-out didn't want to see Dad. Looking into his swimming-pool eyes would have meant contacting his abysmal loneliness and desperation, accepting his pain. Anguish would ooze from his jaw, his mouth, the softness of his hands. It would coat my joints and dreams, and I couldn't afford that. I was attempting an escape from what I'd always assumed was my destiny; that is, a life of scurrying and dragging and moving on. I had in mind an ascension, a real transformation—from illegitimate to legitimate—and it was going to take stamina and a modicum of self-deception. My father's sadness would work like a cement shoe. Viewing his defeat firsthand would sink my bright, new future.

The admissions office at the University of Minnesota was beige and intimidating. I was assigned to a harried, middle-aged man with glasses and a dark mustache. He examined my application with skepticism: dropped out of high school, got Fs and Ds throughout eleventh grade, no parental financial support. I explained that I'd applied for a Pell grant and fully expected to qualify. He was unimpressed. I said my aim was to start at the College of Liberal Arts in the fall. He asked if I'd consider General College, which I knew to be a swamp for murky kids with shitty records who were expected to drop out in a year. I pointed out my GED scores, which, he admitted, showed a tiny spark of promise. I asked to take a college placement test. Sighing, he passed me the sign-up papers as if tossing a dollar to a bum.

I did well on the test, and my Pell grant came through, largely due to the fact that Dad's income was zero. (For pity points, I'd jotted on the application's margin, "He's in prison.") I was admitted to the College of Liberal Arts for the upcoming quarter. Fuck you, mustache man.

August 31, 1987

Jennifer,

How have you been, honey? Thought I'd take time out from my busy schedule to drop you a line. Are you all signed up for school? I haven't heard from you lately so I didn't know if you still planned to enter the ivied halls or not.

I don't know if I told you, but I'm enrolled at the U. of Wisc. and start next week. I'm taking a creative writing class and thought I might pick up a few pointers for my book. You never can tell . . . Is everything O.K. with you? I worry about you when I don't get any cards or letters. You always appear so happy-go-lucky and cheerful, and I wonder if you really are . . .

If you don't make it over here in the near future would you write and let me know what's happening? One of these days I'll write you a long letter.

I miss you.

Love, Dad
Write?

Since his incarceration, my father had taken up writing, an art worthy of all the attention and obsession he had to burn. Locked in his cell at night, he pecked away at a manual Olivetti. Typing was almost like talking to somebody; through sentences and paragraphs, he exorcised all the swirling thoughts and suspicions, his anxious creativity. Dad had lots of literary ideas, most of them overly clever and lacking emotional grip. He attempted a children's book called *Graham Quacker* (ducks, for whatever reason, were a recurring theme) and various other stories, short and long. Finally he settled on the project that would consume the better part of his time in prison—*Cash Flow: A Biographical Novel*. The book is about a misunderstood and much maligned oddball kid named Herbert

Roquefort Jensen, who goes on to become filthy rich and stratospherically famous, leaving his former detractors aghast at the shabby way in which they'd treated him. The story is narrated by a character named Herbert Mallard, who, as far as I can ascertain, is actually Herbert Jensen in disguise.

Dad mailed me chapters over the years, which I returned with delicately worded criticisms, such as "too much repetition here?" or "overuse of adjectives—cut?" There were qualities to recommend his writing, mainly its vividness. But, generally, the pages were overwrought and clichéd. I found myself embarrassed by his perverted sense of humor, which contradicted the sophisticated image I still clung to. One passage describes young Herbert wearing a pair of iridescent sharkskin slacks, under which he'd tied a five-pound sausage to his testicles, so that it hung down past his knee. "He really didn't know exactly why he did this," reads *Cash Flow,* "he just did. It probably gave him some kind of a feeling of superiority, he supposed. That, along with the thrill of seeing the wide-eyed looks of amazement among the girls."

Sept. 13, 1987

Jennifer,

I was just reading your much-appreciated letter again and thought I'd write one of my own—one to let you know what's going on in this wonderful place.

Today is a grey and dismal day; it's been raining since dawn, and the rec yard is closed (along with the library and all the other facilities). T.V. tubes throughout the institution have been cleaned and polished in readiness for the myriad of football games due after lunch. My roommate has his radio on and tuned to his favorite country station. Right now, Tanya Tucker is singing some twangy thing through her nose called "You Done Left Me" or something like that.

Talk about depressing.

My roommate just left to go watch football saying as he

went out the door: "I'll leave the radio on for you to listen to, but if you go out, turn it off." Imagine him thinking everybody in the world loves Country Western music!

Click.

I prefer my little walkman radio. I put my earphones on, tune in a little Chopin or Mozart, and shut the world out— and this mob and all the racket. You wouldn't believe the noise in here—it's like living in the monkey house at the zoo. But you get used to it, eventually. I now think a person can get used to anything, or at least tolerate, if he has to, the worst situations imaginable.

I've been typing like crazy—if you can call hunting and pecking and 2-fingering the old Olivetti typing like crazy . . . Anyway, I'm up to page 180 on my book. Only 50 or 60 more pages left to type, then comes the hard part: The rewriting and editing. I should have the whole thing done by the 1st of the year. I've signed up for 2 English courses at the U. of W. here; one is a creative writing course which, after the first class, seems very elementary—very basic, and may not help me after all (here I am so far advanced and I didn't even know it!). Well, at least I can get a critical opinion of my fabulous scribblings from a fairly knowledgeable professor; he has a PHD in Literature and should know what he's talking about. I wonder how overjoyed he'll be when I present him my telephone book–size manuscript. Heh heh.

I know this book ("Cash Flow") could conceivably be printed and put on the market. About the only thing lacking is my use (or lack) of the metaphor—something I've yet to master, and the thing I'm working on now—"You *can* teach an old dog new tricks." See, I've already got a handle on my metaphors.

In your letter you said when you hear from me you know everything is "O.K." Honey, don't you know that as far as you're concerned, everything is always "O.K."?

You needn't write long letters either; just a word or two from you tells *me* everything is O.K. (I guess we feel the same way . . .)

Your picture is not big enough—I want one to hang on my wall! My little girl has become a woman it appears and prettier every day (you don't have any baby fat left on your sweet little kisser!).

I want to tell you how proud I am of you honey. I know it must be traumatic starting college, being on your own, having to worry about money . . . And it must be tough when people ask you about your parents—"What does your father do, Jennifer?" Jesus, what a situation. As far as anyone else is concerned, your father is living in Texas or New Jersey or someplace, O.K.?

Back to school: I think you're making a wise choice going into journalism. It'll be rough at first, re-learning all the basics of sentence structure, punctuation, etc., but I think you have a natural talent (as I've told you 3 or 4,000 times) for observation and seeing things and seeing *into* things, describing feelings, emotions, characters—in other words, you'll make a good writer. I wouldn't be surprised if you turn out to be another Pearl Buck or Gertrude Stein.

Anyway, sweetie, I want to wish you good luck in school and the first step on your way to fame and fortune and accomplishment and fulfillment. It'll be a tough grind, but I know you can do it. If you ever feel like discussing anything, you can always find a sympathetic ear (or in this case I guess it would be sympathetic *eye*) with me, so write.

> I love you so very much,
> Dad

I moved into an apartment located a few blocks from campus, the top floor of a duplex with a screened front porch and sunny bedroom. My new roommate, Beth, was a French teacher and avid baseball fan. She owned two cats that, late at night, galloped at my latched bedroom door attempting to shoulder it open. I hung a few pictures and set out some knickknacks. In a corner of the living room, I set up a desk with pens in a cup and an electric typewriter. It was there I would write my school papers.

Dad, having finally ceased asking me to visit, requested pictures. I decided to create a photo-essay of myself, a day in the life of Jennifer Vogel, enlisting Beth's help to effect the greatest possible degree of realism. She snapped me with my Dutch-boy haircut watering the plants, brushing my teeth, peeking my grinning and soapy head from behind the shower curtain, pretending to be asleep in bed, pretending to type at the typewriter, boiling ramen noodles on the stove. I consoled myself that these photos, which I arranged by hour of the day, were almost as good as a visit.

I'd create another pictorial for Dad in the fall of 1988. Driving to Brainerd, I'd visit the spots we'd enjoyed when I was a kid. It was eerie to return after a decade. I couldn't help viewing the cheery resort town through my father's sulky nostalgia. I stopped by the old cabin, the one he'd constructed from the ashes of the previous dwelling. The woman who answered the door was friendly. She allowed me inside, where I noted every change she and her family had made (*Orange carpeting—how could they!*). I strolled alone to the lake's shore and past the boathouse, which stood as a perfectly preserved monument. My throat tightened. I clicked a dozen shots and drove away. I finished the roll on the way out of town: the blue ox statue at Paul Bunyan Land; the large rock local kids graffitied on; Bar Harbor; the lion's-head drinking fountain; a highway sign that read, "Whoa! You Passed the Pine Beach Road." I wrapped these sad exhibits in a sunny letter and mailed them off to Dad. For some reason, he thanked me.

My days at the University of Minnesota began early. I'd signed up for morning classes in order to make my job at a downtown chocolate shop by two. The campus itself was bright and promising, the windows of its regal brick buildings winking smartly as I passed.

The teachers were distinguished, more concerned with educating than busting class cutters. I even enjoyed the administrative details—the lines, the fat packets that arrived in the mail describing each quarter's options. I sensed a new independence and the smallest inkling of privilege.

At the same time, I found myself elbow to elbow with jocks and geniuses, people with money and confidence. Their faces were inscrutable, absent any marks of trouble. Among them, I felt slovenly, smudged with gray soot, used, irreversibly illegitimate. I knew about stretching a dollar, hitchhiking, and keeping my blanket dry while sleeping outdoors, but I had no idea how to navigate this smiling academic ballet of up-and-comers. I thought of my father and how difficult it must have been for him, sitting in those office chairs in Seattle, trying to convince each golfing HR manager to make the hire. *I'm upbeat! A real team player!*

At Oxford, Dad became embroiled in arguments with the United States Parole Commission. Attempting to bump up his "presumptive parole date," set at June 10, 1991, he protested that the commission had utilized faulty math. He wrote letters accusing them of counting bank robberies he'd never formally been charged with: "When arrested, I thought being honest and 'coming clean' was the right thing to do. Was I naive in believing that?" The commission dismissed my father's reasoning.

His only option was to earn early release, a chore to which he fully committed himself, putting in overtime at his job, completing the prescribed twelve-week alcohol treatment program, masking his contempt. Progress reports describe him as "always courteous and respectful in his dealings with staff," the type who stays out of trouble, a model prisoner who "should be fully employable upon release." This campaign of ingratiation began to pay off when, on October 27, 1987, Dad received his first recommendation for "Meritorious Good Time," based on job performance. Working as a janitor, my father had swept and mopped in a very dependable and industrious manner.

December 15, 1987

Dear Jennifer,

It's kind of a grey, dismal day here (cheerful beginning, huh). I went out walking in the yard this morning and actually made some laps on the jogging track. According to the weather man, there's a big blizzard headed this way, and I thought I'd go out and say goodbye to the grass, which won't be visible again until April.

I watched the Ronny & Mike meeting on television, and though it was mostly pomp and ceremony, I think it's at least a beginning to undo the insane arms build-up. Let's hope public pressure and a little momentum will lead to something meaningful—like total disarmament.

By the time you get this letter, you'll be another year older—how does it feel? Did you get my card? I wish I was able to buy you a new car or a home or something, but I'm a little short right now, honey. Maybe when I'm home again.

—It's about chow time, so I'll have to come back to you later.

Hello again. Just got back from my English class. The professor has now critiqued the first two chapters of my fabulous book and he thinks it's some great stuff. He recommended I delete a few things, though—some superfluous paragraphs & words, but I don't think I will; the areas he thinks should be eliminated are important later on in the story. But, of course, he wouldn't know that since he's only read chapters 1 & 2 . . .

It's been a busy day and I can hardly keep my eyes open. I worked from 7:30 until 2:00, then 2 hours of working out in the gym, followed by school. So if this letter starts to drift off, that's why. I do write some crummy letters, don't I? For some reason I never could write a decent letter—I've always felt so rigid when writing letters, as if I'm reporting some hog prices on the Chicago market.

It's a good thing none of my constriction carries over into my best-selling novel. It's much easier, at least for me, to write about someone other than myself.

Well, sweetie, you take care of yourself (so far you seem to have done an excellent job) and if you get a chance would you talk to Liz? She needs an understanding and sympathetic ear right now.

I love you
I miss you
Happy Birthday!
Merry Christmas!
Dad
Write?

March 30, 1988

Dear Jennifer,

First of all, I would like to tell you what a sweetheart you are. You didn't have to put that money in a joint account with me, honey; it's yours to do with as you please. You probably could use some new spring clothes or a new bike or something. I guess it's not enough for a car. I'm so happy things are going well for you and that you're happy. I'm also very proud of you.

Nothing much has been happening around here, unless you count the melting of the final snow bank a happening. It's finally gone—all of it. Now to get into my spring routine of exercising and jogging and not smoking (again).

The book is coming along nicely, and after I put it aside for a month (to gain some new perspective) I'll go over it one last time. Speaking of books, I hope to be able to read something that my talented daughter Jennifer has written or will write someday. You do have a lot of creativity, you know. I even stole one of your ideas and put it into my piece of fantastic literature.

Nick has started writing to me on a regular basis and I

enjoy hearing from him and his wry wit. Maybe we'll end up being friends after all.

How about writing and letting me know what's going on in your life? You know, it's been almost 2½ years since I've seen your smiling face. I miss you. You don't know what I'd give to be able to put my arms around you and give you a big hug right now.

I love you, Jennifer.

Dad

P.S. If you have a recent spare photo . . .

Sometimes Dad called. He sounded lousy when he did, mainly because he tried so hard to sound cheerful. He was afraid that if he exposed even a corner of bitterness or despair, I wouldn't speak to him again. I made attempts at digging to the center of things, inquiring about his cellmate and how he was sleeping, but he rejected those topics, preferring to talk about my progress at school, what I'd eaten for dinner, the warmth of my clothes, my friends. I was a soft, warm bubble from home; he nuzzled my words, basking in the timbre of a voice with honest-to-God feeling in it. Always in the background was the noise of convicts: people barking and jabbering and slamming doors. Dad had to speak loudly and sometimes cup the phone to fend off a would-be intruder ("Hey! I'm on the list until eleven!"). Then would come the digital operator warning us that only two minutes remained. Then one minute remained. Then thirty seconds remained. Then, amid a flurry of I-love-yous and we'll-talk-again-next-months, we would be cut off.

About two years into his sentence, we established a routine whereby we talked on the first Sunday of each month. Dad would write with the exact time of his call and I'd wait by the phone, lest Beth pick up the line and my father die of embarrassment when the operator announced, "You have a collect call from a federal correctional institution, will you accept the charge?"

I was almost always home when he called. The few times I wasn't, Dad panicked, going so far as to phone Mom asking after my whereabouts. I didn't look forward to these conversations; I answered the line because I felt sorry for him and shitty about not visiting. On the first Sunday of each month, I completed my daughterly duty by making his day and destroying mine. I lay in bed on those afternoons, paralyzed, a brick on my chest, thinking he'd crushed my near-legitimate life. I often dreamed about Dad, even during the day. One morning, in the middle of an American government lecture, I dozed off while taking notes. In my stupor, I imagined the professor was my father. He was educating the class about his campaign, "Gophers Are Rodents."

In a misplaced and surprising burst of civic pride (Dad was no sports fan), he'd once been obsessed with renaming the University of Minnesota sports teams, called the Golden Gophers. Just before we'd departed for Seattle, he ran a newspaper campaign that asked, "Are you sometimes embarrassed by the name Gopher? . . . Imagine, Michigan as the 'Michigan Mice,' or Wisconsin as the 'Wisconsin Weasels.' Does 'Gopher' strike terror in the hearts and minds of opponents? Of course not! Why not the Minnesota Timber Wolves or the Minnesota Moose . . . Anything but a rodent which you may have run over on the way to the game."

He created "Gophers Are Rodents" bumper stickers and lapel pins featuring a deceased gopher on its back, a daisy in its clutches, Xs in place of eyes. He sold them for $3 each. Years later, when the U of M beefed up the image of its mascot—they turned it into a weight-lifting gopher—my father took credit.

April 24, 1988

Jennifer,

I'm sitting here trying not to think of roasted, toasted, aromatic cigarettes; I quit again, this time for good. It's been 4 days and I think (hope) I'm just about over the withdrawal— I'm a nervous wreck.

Congrats on your excellent marks at Gopher U (as in I Gopher U). I'm really *proud* of you, honey. It's always so nice to hear from you; I really enjoy reading what you've been doing from day to day, at work, school, etc. It makes me feel closer to you. Don't ever think describing your average day will bore me. By the way, I'm enclosing an excerpt from my book's first draft. I've changed some of it in the latest version, but it's essentially the same. Let me know what you think. Oh, and don't show it to anybody else (authorial paranoia—you know how it is, thinking others will steal your ideas). And speaking of paranoia, the protagonist in this incredible little tale is a real basket case (as you may judge for yourself from the enclosed).

You will notice certain point-of-view changes, some authorial intrusion with an unusual amount of empathy shown toward the hero. All part of what I'm trying to establish. All of the incidents, no matter how far-out or weird or one-track, are pertinent to the story and will become apparent in the last chapter. All of it is fictitious, and if something seems off-beat or strange it was meant to be, to make the hero sound strange. It is also all a product of the imagination.

Guess what? I finally had a BLT sandwich—the first one in almost 2½ years. Made it myself. Ingredients included: toast from breakfast, a tomato appropriated from the kitchen, and lettuce from the noon-meal salad bar. Unfortunately, I was unable to obtain mayonnaise; I had to use one of those little packets of salad dressing (1000 Island). The BLT was just O.K. Of course, what can you expect with no Miracle Whip? The whole concoction was heated on top of my light fixture.

Are you still planning to go down for Liz's graduation? Let me know when you'll be there and I'll call. I thought I'd get Liz a ring for a graduation present, maybe an amethyst, which is her birthstone. I talked to Cheryl and she said she could get me a good deal on one through her jewelry store connections. If you would call her right away and give her what you think Liz's ring size is we can get the ball rolling. You and Liz have about the same hands (both delicate & beautiful) & ring size, so your size should fit her, don't you think? Cheryl will get it engraved and I thought you could give it to Liz when you go to Iowa.

I miss you.

Write back soon.

Love, Dad

Since returning to Minneapolis, I'd made regular treks to Iowa for Christmas. I hauled my suitcase and garbage bag of wrapped gifts downtown and boarded the midnight Greyhound that dropped me in Iowa around 4:30 A.M. Mom braved hours driving along dark, ice-covered highways to retrieve me from the bus station.

Just before Christmas 1988—mere months after Dad, once again, had been deemed a "quiet, cooperative individual" whose "overall institutional adjustment . . . has been very good," and only weeks after he, once again, had been denied an earlier parole date— I exited the bus at the usual station, which was closed. I crouched against the small building in the gray lamplight with my bag of presents, waiting for Mom. The sack contained two extra-special gifts for Nick and Liz, from Dad. Somewhere along the way, I'd become his emissary to the rest of the family. I provided updates to all parties, mended fences, did PR. I'd mailed Nick and Liz pages from his book, which I'd signed "Dad" in an accurate imitation of his penmanship. His memory was on life support.

At the house, Mom fixed ham-and-cheese sandwiches. Buffy, our childhood dog, stood swaying in the middle of the dining room floor. She was blind with cataracts. The doorways were layered with scales of Christmas cards. The artificial tree sparkled with colored lights, red bulbs, and tinsel. It felt nice to be home.

On Christmas Eve we drank pink champagne and made a late,

drunken effort at caroling. We opened gifts: boxes of chocolates, scarves, salon shampoo. Then I handed Nick and Liz the packages from Dad.

"Hmm, what's this?" Nick shook his with a feigned look of shock.

"It's a gift from Dad. Open it."

He and Liz unwrapped their presents at the same time.

Dad had mailed me $200, obtained from where I didn't know, asking that I give $100 each to Nick and Liz. At the bank, I exchanged the large bills for two hundred singles. I then crinkled each dollar like something organic—lettuce or kale—and filled two red Chinese food containers. I was proud of the idea. It was clever, worthy of Dad, and I assumed they'd be touched by his thoughtfulness.

Nick and Liz dumped out the boxes and started counting. Nick finished first and complained that his was $1 short.

October 1989

Dear Jennifer,

Well, another exciting weekend has come and gone. Each one that goes by means that much less time remaining. It would be nice if they'd go by a little faster however.

The trees have finally turned here; they're not very bright, kind of brown and rusty-looking. Must be all oaks. Kind of typifies this place—drab, solid. I'm glad winter is coming, though, the time really rushes by. I guess that's because of the short days and all the time spent indoors reading, writing, and watching the boob tube.

Your birthday card was beautiful. Thank you for remembering, honey. And thank you for writing; your letters always cheer me up. One of the few pleasures in here is hearing my name called at mail-call and getting one of your beautiful letters. And then reading it and finding everything is alright with you. And that you're happy; that especially pleases me.

After I talked to you last week I kept thinking about the Chinese food and the prime rib you mentioned. When I get back to Mpls. my immediate itinerary as far as gorging myself on longed-for food will look something like this:

1. Prime rib, baked potato w/sour cream and maybe a little red wine
2. Lobster. Side dishes not necessary
3. Chinese: Moo goo gai pan, tung goo gai kow, sweet & sour shrimp, maybe a little wan fu
4. A good pizza
5. A good burger
6. A chocolate malt and a BLT at Bridgeman's
7. Fresh-baked pastry: glazed donuts, strawberry pie, etc., etc., etc., etc., etc., etc., etc.
8. Walleye-pike (maybe at the Mariner in Mendota— where you and I ate several times)
9. Barbecue ribs—at Rudolphs?
10. Fresh caramel corn—warm
11. More prime rib
12. More lobster
13. More Chinese
14. All of the above in the company of you

It's funny how just writing this stuff down makes your mouth water. I could've thought up some more food items but it would only have made me hungrier, hungryer? More hungry.

> I miss you.
> And *love* you very much.
> Dad

P.S. I think about you all the time and what a sweetheart you are.

The further I progressed in college, the less I wanted to think about Dad. I'd managed, through accomplishment and selective amnesia, to ground down the past into a fine powder. I'd been hatched at nineteen, as far as I was concerned. *Grew up poor? I don't know what you're talking about. A father in prison? What?* I'd successfully transmogrified the isolating fixtures of pain and disillusionment into the loud, bond-friendly tenants of activism. The qualities that had rendered me a miserable, insomniac child would make me a good journalist. I was well equipped to travel light, look ahead, and fight hard.

On the strength of the blindingly idealistic letter I wrote to the School of Journalism, I was formally admitted into the professional program in time for the fall quarter in 1989 and was even awarded a small scholarship. I fared well, while working two jobs, and finally mustered the courage to apply for a reporter's position at the Minnesota *Daily*, the U of M student newspaper. I was hired as a cops reporter and found daily journalism fairly easy. Sometimes I wrote three or four stories a day.

While my life was on the upswing, Dad's continued to dribble down the drain. He mentioned his fast-approaching release date, but didn't seem able to focus on the details. Maybe he'd work for his brother Tom or for Cheryl's husband. He suggested that he might even "look up old Molly" who "wasn't so bad, now that I really think about it." Unfortunately, weeks after this utterance, my father discovered that Molly, whom he'd financially drained and then abandoned without a word, had committed suicide. She'd swallowed a handful of pills at her parents' house, to which she'd retreated, on her fortieth birthday.

Dad's prison sentence had paralleled almost exactly the term of my college education. The learning processes we'd undergone were diametrically opposed. I'd gained so much, while he'd only lost. I dreaded seeing him. I wanted to help him, but I didn't want to love him.

In late 1990, my father made a final attempt at early release. A demonstration that he'd accomplished "superior programming" during his nearly five-year incarceration would shave an additional four months from his sentence. He marshaled significant resources in buttressing his argument to the Parole Commission. The most emphatic support came from Gary Faga, Oxford prison's staff librarian. In a letter dated September 24, he wrote:

> Inmate John B. Vogel, number 04788-085, has worked for me in the institution library for 3½ years. Prior to his arrival, the library had been operated exclusively by Oxford staff and by University of Wisconsin-Baraboo contract personnel. Because John has done such an outstanding job, assisting staff and inmates, working mainly unsupervised, we created a position for him, that of Inmate Library Clerk.
>
> In this position he continues to demonstrate his reliability, trustworthiness, and especially his industriousness, by working long hours, day and night, six days per week. *In 3½ years he has not missed a single day of work.* . . .
>
> John was also instrumental in drafting the Library Services Guidelines, now in use at the BOP Training Center in Denver as an instruction manual and conceptual planning guide in establishing new prison libraries and in standardizing existing facilities. . . .
>
> Even though his position in the Education Department and the library is not one where outstanding performance is generally recognized . . . I feel he has done such a commendable job that he has earned something, and I would like to submit him for consideration for a Superior Programming Award. In all my 14 years at Oxford, I haven't known an inmate more deserving. He is truly an exceptional individual, an individual who has had a positive influence on the Education Department, the library, and on the Education staff. We hate to lose him.

In November 1990—the same month I started working as a reporter for *City Pages* and just a few months before I finished college—the

Parole Commission granted Dad the superior programming award. His parole date was moved up from June 10 to February 10, 1991, "with the special alcohol aftercare condition." The last six weeks of his sentence would be spent at a Minneapolis halfway house.

By Christmas, he'd be out.

18

It wasn't Norman Rockwell's malt shop

IWAS PARKED OUTSIDE the squat, stucco Volunteers of America halfway house, just down the block from Kmart on Lake Street in a busted-out part of Minneapolis. The sun glared bright off the snow, glinting through the frosted windshield of my baby blue Rent-a-Wreck. Four days before Christmas, it was the kind of crisp, naked winter morning that shatters metal and exposes every crack on a face. Dad had fought hard to gain release in time for the holiday he'd always dreaded, so we could spend it together. He'd been set free—allowed to stroll through the heavy doors into the air like it was nothing—on the previous afternoon. He'd boarded a Greyhound. Now he was on Lake Street.

I wore my favorite outfit: black pants, white blouse, blue wool jacket, new bra. I'd even applied red lipstick, as if Dad were a lost lover. I examined my face in the rearview mirror and wondered whether he'd recognize me. Would he think I'd turned out all right? He'd requested that I remain in the car, that I not come to the door, in deference to whom or what I wasn't sure. I waited. A young black woman walked by in a parka, dragging a child by the arm. The caterwauling boy refused to move his legs. I waited.

Finally, my father stepped from the building. He squinted down at the pavement: gray sweatshirt, tan pants, flimsy gray jacket. No gloves. I looked at him, the first eyes from the past. His skin was pale, his hair thin and the color of road salt. He walked toward the car in a hunch. He was forty-eight, but looked eighty. Had he shrunk? Or had I fashioned him taller in my mind?

Our eyes caught, breath, recognition. His mouth smiled at me through the windshield. We embraced across bucket seats until tears welled up. He didn't want to let go. I longed to run. I felt sorry for him, the way you do a stranger. His circumstances were suddenly devastating to me.

"Look at you! Honey, you're beautiful."

"You look good yourself." I lied. "I wondered whether you'd know me. It's been so long."

"You're all grown up."

"Yes."

"I'd know you anywhere. Of course I would. You're my little girl."

"I've thought about you so much." I wanted to apologize for not visiting, but instead asked, "Are you okay?"

"Oh, yeah, I'm just super." Sarcasm, a good sign.

"Are you—"

"Hey, would you mind if we got the hell out of here?"

The car's defrost was broken, so Dad valiantly went to work scraping the inside of the windshield with an ID card. Peels of frost fell to the dash. I had a big, restorative day planned. We'd eat lunch at a hamburger joint called Bridgeman's ("6. A chocolate malt and a BLT at Bridgeman's") and dinner at this Chinese place I knew on Excelsior Boulevard ("3. Chinese: Moo goo gai pan, tung goo gai kow, sweet & sour shrimp, maybe a little wan fu"). His top cravings—numbers one, prime rib, and two, lobster—would have to wait for plusher times. Before lunch, we'd shop for clothes. Dad had only $159.50 to his name, but I'd drained the $1,000 from the joint account I'd opened for him a few years earlier.

First, we cruised through downtown, so my father could marvel at all that had changed and, hopefully, notice all that remained exactly and comfortingly the same. The shop windows were decorated in gold and red. Santas with bells stood on corners exhaling white puffs. Dad watched in silence. I pulled into the parking lot of a discount clothing store.

"What's this?"

"Let's get you out of those clothes."

"I don't—"

"Come on. Let's buy a nice sweater and pants."

"I guess we could look."

We browsed up and down the aisles, but he refused every item I chose. He wouldn't try anything on. I couldn't fathom why he wasn't leaping from his prison drabs, exuberantly shedding the past five years. He seemed stuck, clinging to the familiar amid people and places grown more assaultive since his last encounter. He suggested that we move on, come back to clothing later. He apologized, and I had the nerve to act hurt.

At Bridgeman's, I chose a booth by the window, thinking he'd had enough of walls and would relish a view of the street. But he was fidgety and miserable. He couldn't look our waitress in the eye and was afraid to ask for salt or even the location of the pay phone. The man across the table from me was small and broken. I realized prison had robbed him of his most precious asset: the ability to charm. No longer could he rely on the allegiance of strange women or orchestrate situations to his advantage. He felt entitled to nothing. The father I'd known was dead.

He was still dressed in his prison clothes when I picked him up at the halfway house on Christmas morning. This time he was sitting on the front steps with a man who, upon my arrival, got up and walked inside.

"Boy, this car is a real luxury deal."

"Yeah, it's pretty bad."

"We Vogels have come a long way."

"At least it's got a radio."

I found some Christmas carols so we wouldn't have to speak. I parked in front of Cheryl's apartment building while Dad double-checked the address on a piece of paper. The car chugged a few times after I switched off the ignition. Then, just as my father and I shoved open our doors, he turned and touched my arm.

"Remember, I've been living in Seattle this whole time. I had a business that went bust. That's why I'm back."

The breath ran out of me.

We sat around a big wooden table set fancy for dinner with Cheryl, my cousins, and a few other people. Dad drank vodka and spun gigantic lies about his failed business. He'd returned to Minnesota only to get back on his feet, he said. He'd storm the West again. He talked and talked, but the lies were unconvincing—I mean, he had no money, no car, no gloves, only those prison clothes—and I marveled that he could be so deluded as to think he was fooling anybody. It was force of habit: he'd always defined what the truth was, and if you didn't believe, well, that simply wasn't his problem.

I called Nick, Liz, and Mom from the phone in Cheryl's bedroom. I wanted to be home in Iowa with my hard-up, alcoholic family. It was warm there, with presents and pot roast. I talked for a while, then fetched Dad. I announced him gaily ("Guess who I've got here! Someone who'd really, really like to talk to you!"). We all pretended to be thrilled at his return. I was having one of the worst days of my life.

For his Christmas gift, I gave him a sweater. He opened it and tossed it aside with a wink. When I got up to refill my wineglass, one of Cheryl's daughters cornered me in the kitchen: "Was John really in Seattle these last few years?"

Since Dad's sentence technically didn't expire until February 10, he spent every night for six weeks at the halfway house. During the days, he made moves toward adjustment: He applied for a library card and had a couple of nagging kidney stones removed. With the $1,000, he purchased an old sedan.

I did my best to avoid him. We shared the occasional lunch or dinner—still no lobster or prime rib—during which I checked his progress and offered pointers on acting normal. But his needs weighed heavily. He phoned nearly every day. On my answering machine, his voice sounded ominous and demanding: JENNIFER, THIS IS YOUR FATHER. CALL ME. Click.

In mid-February, Liz came up from Iowa for her birthday. Dad insisted on driving her to the Minneapolis–St. Paul airport for a soda and hamburger. While in prison, he'd grown fond of the sit-com *Cheers,* and the airport had constructed a working replica of the fabled Boston watering hole, complete with life-size mechanical models of Norm and Cliff seated at the end of the bar. Liz and Dad sat side by side, as if these were the good old days, as if the airport was Paul Bunyan Land or the lion's-head drinking fountain. Except Liz was too old and too smart for such simple illusions. The outing was uncomfortable, and when Dad insisted on paying the tab with his crumpled dollar bills it crossed into pitiful.

We were on our way back to south Minneapolis from Cheryl's, where we'd eaten Liz's birthday dinner. It was late and Dad, who'd had a few drinks, was driving and talking. He was careening into one of his ugly rants about niggers, how they didn't contribute anything to society except loud talk and unwanted babies. As he'd settled into freedom, he'd hardened, become mean. "How in the hell can they be so cute when they're kids?" He was getting wildly worked up when I stepped onto the tracks before his speeding train. I couldn't take any more of it.

"Oh, and you've contributed so much!" I yelled.

The accusation hung there. Liz crouched in the backseat. With one sentence, I'd shattered the illusion of a lifetime. The fable that cast him as the respectable father and me as the loyal daughter, the two of us as peas in a pod, was gone, destroyed. He turned to face me, his eyes burning black as the devil's. There was no love in them. He screamed, "So, now I know what you really think!"

We talked by phone a few weeks later. He'd smashed the car. He needed money. He urged me to sign on to a new joint bank account. I had to get out. I explained that at this particular time, I couldn't handle having him in my life. He claimed to understand. He asked me to check in periodically, to let him know that I was okay. I promised to. And never did.

Dad was replaced by a recurrent dream. It began with the stark realization that I was to spend the rest of my life in prison. I'd done something wrong, but I didn't know what and that didn't seem to be the point anyway. I panicked at the impending loss: never again would I eat good food or sleep entangled with a warm body. Then I reasoned with myself. Prison wouldn't be so bad. I'd have plenty of time to read and write and exercise. I wouldn't have to pay rent or live up to expectations of any sort. I always awoke before coming to terms with my fate, my heart pounding and my head racing with what seemed a genuine understanding of what prison feels like. It was as if Dad had cast a curse.

The dreams eventually became so severe that, for the first time in my life, I went to a psychiatrist. Months in his chair—confession, hypnosis—and the best he could come up with was that there was something inside me I was afraid of.

19

June 1995

IT HAD BEEN NEARLY five months since Dad had gone on the lam, and not a single word. Spring had arrived with its usual optimism, baseball, budding leaves, and barbecue grills. I glanced around at the green, the slanted sunlight, the squirrels fucking, and I couldn't feel him anymore. He had been gone so much of my life, but this gone felt different than the gones before. It was ominous. Something broken, if not dead.

The marshals continued to talk to family and friends, while the Secret Service scanned the country's money flow for hundred-dollar bills printed with Dad's serial numbers. There had been nothing. Then, suddenly, appearing like a trail of bread crumbs, my father's handiwork surfaced in Ohio, Kentucky, Indiana, North Dakota. The last turned up in West Fargo, a town within fleeing distance of the Canadian border and only eighty-five miles from the Minnesota town where his friend Jimmy lived. Kawaters checked dates, tried to decipher a pattern. He thought my father might have hooked up with a traveling carnival.

Reports relating to the marshals' Fargo operation are cryptic. One, dated July 7, from the office in Minneapolis to the one in Fargo, reads, "We have asked the secret service agent to re-contact the store employees . . . If it's ok with you—we would like to send a couple of people up for the opening of the Fair—a little surveillance before interviewing any of the carnival workers." The police didn't know whether my father was in Fargo. Counterfeit can be slow to surface. He might have ducked into Canada or gotten all the way to Mexico. Later, Agent Kawaters would marvel at Dad's cunning, or luck. He'd tell the press, "It's almost like he fell off the face of the earth for six months."

The *Unsolved Mysteries* episode kept running through my head. The character in the checkered jacket hadn't seemed like Dad, yet he'd done all those stupid things. He'd been arrested after a string of feebleminded blunders: acting suspicious at the mailing counter, including cocaine in the package, addressing the box to his shop, for Christ's sake, drying fake $100s out in the open, preserving practice bills in his storage locker. These were dumb acts. Yet my father wasn't dumb. Even crazy and paranoid after prison, he'd been cautious. Cautious out of defeat.

The only rationale I could come up with was that perhaps he'd been ruined to the point of actually wishing to be caught. Maybe his had been a willful pattern of carelessness.

There hadn't been much for Dad after leaving Oxford prison. He had a girlfriend for a while, but the romance didn't last. After that, he was alone. He couldn't even fall back on old loves. Molly was dead and it was practically his fault. Debbie was too fine to subject to his pathetic state. He found himself wedged in the bosom of his family, whom he'd never regarded generously. He moved into his brother Tom's apartment, but the friction became unbearable and Tom asked him to leave.

For a few months after, he rented a room at the Hopkins House, a hotel frequented by keg-guzzling partyers, located just up the road from the town house we shared when I first moved to Minneapolis. Then, finally, he settled in with Cheryl at the Bryantwood apartments. Cheryl tried to fashion the most normal life possible, but her brother was beyond reach. Every event was a disappointment. Each reward was too long coming. When Dad made his favorite tapioca pudding on the stove, he couldn't wait for it to finish cooking and gobbled it raw. His heart and hatred were laid bare, with little hope to temper them. He flamed out of all proportion.

In June 1992, a sweet-faced, five-year-old Minneapolis girl disappeared, leaving behind only a bloody sundress and pair of underwear. Dad became obsessed with the case. He wept before the television. His heart sopped each detail—after all, who was more deserving of sympathy than a harmless, loving little girl? When it was revealed that the main suspect had once drunkenly crawled into bed with the girl, my father shook his fist and swore he'd kill the man. Dad had a similarly bizarre response to the TV show *Designing Women*. Each week, when Cheryl settled into her comfy chair to watch the program, her brother slipped into lunacy. At the sight of Anthony Bouvier, the show's black character (who plays, predictably, an endearing ex-con), he hopped about the living room, scratching his armpits and screeching. He banged on the television until Cheryl feared he'd break it.

And on birthdays and Father's Days and Christmases, he sat by the telephone waiting intently for me or Nick or Liz to call. None of us did.

One day, in September 1992, he set aside his pride and contacted me. Actually, he called Mom and asked that she have me mail him a bundle of old photos and letters. I still had them, remnants of the packing job I'd performed in Seattle. I missed Dad, the old Dad, at least the idea of him, but managed to quell those feelings. Besides, I understood the request for the photos to be a matter of temperature taking, a ploy to get me to call or write. The indirectness, the inherent self-pity in this chosen route angered me. I packed the pictures of cabins and sunny days and grade-school papers into a Code West shoe box and slipped in a cool note: *Mom said you wanted this stuff. Take care, Jennifer.* After receiving the package, Dad phoned Mom. He blamed her for turning me against him. He described me as the coldest bitch he'd ever known.

My father had exited prison with a veteran's knowledge of counterfeiting. He'd learned the trade working in the graphics shop at

the federal correctional institution in Phoenix. One of my father's
inmate buddies explained the setup to police. He said Dad was
taught by one of the finest counterfeiters on record. According to
the man's statement,

> [blank] was assigned to the print shop which was a small room
> in the education dept. It contained one small press and we
> would all go down to this shop and John Vogel was very intent
> on learning to counterfeit and [blank] would explain how he
> would first print the fibers on the paper and he went on to train
> John . . . I was not all that intent on learning the aspects of coun-
> terfeiting but we were all friends.
>
> John and I would talk about sailing the world and that he
> wanted to be transferred out of Phoenix to get closer visits with
> his [blank], I believe it was. He talked of counterfeiting and I
> suggested exchanging bogus bills in the border town in Tex,
> Mexico area because they have a lot of Casa de Cambios there
> and it would be easier.

Prison staffers apparently hadn't noticed the illicit training ses-
sions. Nor had they considered it untoward assigning a convicted
counterfeiter to their print shop. Officials, in fact, had been excep-
tionally pleased with the man's progress in teaching my father.
Dad's new skills were trumpeted in a December 8, 1986, memo
from William Sabin, Phoenix's assistant supervisor of education.

> Inmate John Vogel was assigned to the Education Department
> in September, 1986, at which time he was given the duties of
> assisting our lead offset printer, and concurrently learning his
> trade. Since that time, Inmate Vogel has demonstrated an
> exceptional learning ability, having acquired extensive skills in
> the printing craft.
>
> This department's print shop is properly equipped to teach
> hands-on offset printing. The practice and procedures associ-

ated with this trade require extensive study, and the willingness to work many hours beyond those normally scheduled for inmate workers. In this regard, Inmate Vogel has proven himself to be a willing and capable student, with the conscientiousness and drive needed to succeed in this trade craft.

Inmate Vogel expresses an interest in further learning in the Graphic Arts field during the period of his incarceration, and thereby acquiring an employable skill in the printing and graphic arts field at the time of his release. It is felt that his positive attitude and demonstrated success to date will ensure his success in this desire.

Dad had barely been out two months when he'd purchased City Center Printing, the one-horse shop in the Navarre strip mall. (He would change the name to City Centre, in homage to his hometown, Sauk Centre.) The arrangement had been generous—Dad was required to put up only $60 in cash, with monthly payments following. The business came with one steady printing client. Dad scooped up a few more contracts along the way, but not enough to make City Centre a success. Frankly, he wasn't trying very hard: After his arrest, Paula Larson, coproprietor of nearby Larson Printing, told newspapers, "We never, ever came up against him in a bid. Being two miles away from him, we thought that was weird. He had this dungy-looking, back-alley entrance to this hole-in-the-wall print shop. We never understood how he could be in business."

To Dad, counterfeiting was an artistic endeavor. The more perfect the bills, the wealthier he'd become and the less risk there would be of getting caught. It sounded easy. Easier than earning a legitimate living, anyway. He'd already tried that, and failed. Now he was dogged by a felony record and five years wasted in prison. The best he could have hoped for was a slow stream of crummy print jobs that paid shit, forcing him to live in Cheryl's apartment for the rest of his life. Counterfeiting was the answer, all right. He gathered the plate negatives and paper, maybe from Mexico. He practiced late into the night.

Yet, several years into it, his checking account balance still hovered near zero, occasionally dipping into overdraft territory. Bill by bill, he passed his meticulously crafted artwork at Wal-Marts from Minnesota to Florida, each time facing the disingenuous greeter at the door, the gum-snapping teenaged clerk, the chance that someone would notice a slightly odd shade of green or some indescribable something and alert a manager. He'd passed only $50,000 worth and he'd done it alone, slowly, holding his breath, $100 at a time. He trusted nobody to help him.

My father must have realized that, in the end, he wasn't going to make it illegitimately, either. Sure, he'd talked with Jimmy about purchasing the Harbor Inn in northern Minnesota. And there is evidence that he'd stepped up the laundering in order to generate the down payment. But it wouldn't have worked. Maniacally obsessive and hot-tempered, Jimmy was crazier than Dad. He would have made a lousy business partner. No, a move north would only have been a circumstantial adjustment, which wouldn't have changed the inside of Dad's head. Geography wouldn't have altered the fact that society had turned against him and that when he looked at people, they didn't look back.

Still, the worst possible misery wouldn't have convinced my father to return to prison—I knew that—even if it did mean free rent, plenty of reading and writing and workout time, and no expectations of any sort. He wasn't one of those ex-cons who throws a brick through a window in order to sabotage his freedom and return to a familiar setting. He'd hated prison. Hated it. Prison had destroyed him. He said he'd rather die than go back.

Perhaps, I thought. But what if he'd gotten himself arrested to suit an even darker purpose? I considered that there was a longer, more grand trajectory to trace, the full arc of his life, which seemed destined to end in one place only. Suicide.

Dad had talked about it before, usually in passing, a reference to how "everybody would be better off without me" or "maybe I'll just end it." Mainly, he said these things to rally support against killing himself. He teetered. Never had he possessed the courage to give it a real try. Yet, for him, day-to-day living had been excruciating.

It was evinced in his eyes. Melancholy, fear, gray-blue hieroglyphs detailing the missteps of a lifetime. Death was woven into his being; the way he slouched in a chair while the ash grew on his cigarette, the manner in which he preserved pain for future use, the ferocity with which he hunted for open windows and trapdoors. He possessed that volatile combination of self-pity and vengefulness. He mined courage from the secret knowledge that if backed tightly enough into a corner, he could always perform the greatest of escapes. Like Houdini, he'd slip free of his restraints and vanish, leaving only the sagging straitjacket. Cozying up to death this way allowed him to tolerate situations that otherwise would have been unbearable. Because at least he was alive. And tomorrow he could always off himself. Dad told a prison counselor that he'd often considered suicide, especially during the years leading up to the Spokane bank robberies, but he'd refrained because of the anguish it would have caused me, Nick, and Liz.

It took more than the prospect of tearful faces to keep him alive, however. Despite a generally pessimistic outlook, Dad held tightly to a tiny, silken thread of hope. In his mind, there was always the chance things would turn around. The insurance company would believe the cabin had burned by accident, he'd receive a handmade Father's Day card, he'd witness the splendor of the Ulm Pishkun buffalo jump. He'd fall in love.

I wondered whether that gossamer thread had snapped. If so, he'd certainly backed himself into a proper corner. I remembered that, just after being arrested in 1986, he'd told the Spokane police he'd purchased the .38 pistol from an ad in a newspaper without knowing why exactly. He'd just wanted it around. When he'd phoned me at Anita's a few weeks before, he'd said, "If anything should happen to me, I love you." He'd sounded distinctly like someone saying farewell. And I'd thought suicide. I'd even asked. Then there was the bouquet of flowers he'd bought me before robbing the second bank and engaging in the high-speed chase. Had he intended to kill himself if caught? Had he lost the nerve?

If Dad was still alive, it was because he was making preparations, readying himself for something big. I was sure of it. Because that's what it would take: the massaging of memories, the nursing of pain, the steadying of will, and the creation of a set of dramatic, inescapable circumstances. His end would not be quiet or private, so-called dignified. He would orchestrate his fate—the logical finale to the public circus he began the day he mailed the Brownsville package. Hell, decades before that. My father never thought himself deserving of the ordinary. He would show me. He would show the world the greatness, the heart, the absolute genius that nobody had appreciated while he was around. And we'd all cry and for years after feel sorry for the shabby manner in which we'd treated him.

There are plenty of ways to kill oneself: pills, drowning, jumping, shooting, hanging, carbon monoxide, Drano, a plastic bag over the head, a razor blade to the wrist, strychnine, nails driven into the skull, oven gas, even hara-kiri. Sometimes those who've obsessed on the details long enough—Freud equated the passion for suicide with being in love—create wholly unique methods. The idea is that, given the range of options, each suicide, in some way, reflects the life that preceded it. If this was true, then Dad's end would be violent and spectacular.

20

July 1995

AT 12:23 P.M. ON July 12, Dad emerged from hiding.
On that blistering Wednesday afternoon, at the
height of the day's heat, my father strolled through the glass front
doors of the stark, cement American Federal Bank on West Forty-
first Street in Sioux Falls, South Dakota. He wore a gray shirt, tan
pants, brown shoes, a baseball cap, and sunglasses. He looked plain.
In fact, he appeared so run-of-the-mill that Angie May, the teller on
duty at the time, thought she recognized him as a regular. She didn't
notice his disposable painter's gloves or the pistol tucked in his
waistband.

Besides May and a few other employees, Dad was the only person in the bank, unusual for the noon hour on a workday. He
approached May's window, pointed the gun, and tossed over a couple of plastic shopping bags. One of them fluttered to the floor.
He didn't bother with small talk. "I'm here to make a withdrawal,"
he said. May noted that my father seemed calm. She was certain he
wouldn't kill her as long as she did what he asked. And that was
the bank's policy, anyway: Give up the money. Don't be a hero.

American Federal VP Steve Christianson could see May's station
from his office. Something was amiss. May was acting nervous. He
saw her step back from the teller window. When he got up from his
desk, as he later told the press, "I saw he had a gun and thought, 'uh-

oh, this is serious.'" Dad said to May, "I'm not going to hurt you, but just give me your large bills." That's when Christianson approached, a captain apparently willing to go down with the ship. My father shifted focus to Christianson, instructing him to "go to the vault and get all the large bills." Christianson followed orders. He and May briskly stuffed a shopping bag with money and handed it to Dad. Dad snatched it up and walked out the door, casual as you please.

However, there was a hitch. While my father was gathering his bounty, a customer had entered the bank, one R. A. "Shade" Essem, the fifty-three-year-old proprietor of Essem Refrigeration. Essem noticed that May, his friend and frequent teller, was in trouble. He sized up my father, drew a bead on the situation. When Dad exited the bank, Essem followed.

Dad strode toward the Olds, stationed across the street in the parking lot of the Lonestar Steakhouse & Saloon. He opened the door and got in. Pulling off the hat and glasses—the minimal disguise—he straightened his hair in the rearview mirror. Essem watched, then hopped into his four-wheel-drive pickup, intent on pursuing.

The two met on the way out of the parking lot. Dad maneuvered quickly, pulling into the street just ahead of an oncoming car, but Essem stuck close and copied down a description of the Olds, including its license plate number. As they proceeded, police cars passed, sirens blaring, cherries rolling. They were headed the wrong way, toward the bank. Essem flashed his headlights and honked his horn, but none of the officers noticed. On his cell phone, he dialed the police department. Busy. So he noted Dad's route, double-checked the plate number, and sped back to the bank. By the time he got there, the cops had pulled over some other shlub.

That spring and summer, Sioux Falls had experienced a rash of bank robberies—sixteen within several months. The townspeople were frustrated. The police were offended. Later, after Essem had officially been declared a hero by the good people of Sioux Falls (he'd receive $1,000, a Certificate of Appreciation, and his smiling mug in the local paper), he told the press, in true vigilante fashion, "It's going to keep happening if people don't keep their eyes open and help each other out. If it isn't done, these guys are going to override the city."

Sioux Falls is situated in the southeast corner of South Dakota, just a few miles from the borders of Minnesota and Iowa. It's flat country. The roads run stick-straight. They follow property lines and the edges of neatly planted corn and soybean and alfalfa fields. They border pastures of pigs and cows, pacing and eating and shitting morning till night. They traverse slight hills embedded with stones and sparse clumps of craggy trees. The intersections of these narrow, tidy byways form an endless web of squares and rectangles within squares and rectangles within squares and rectangles. And at the crease of it all, like a sharp fold in the scenery, rests the horizon, which brings into relief every building and standing creature. You can spot trouble coming from miles away.

Dad proceeded out of town. He hopped onto Interstate 229, which loops around Sioux Falls and connects to the long ribbon of I-90. He obeyed all traffic laws, keeping to the speed limit, signaling when changing lanes, riding perfectly between the lines. He cleared the entrance ramp onto eastbound I-90. Nobody was following.

Meanwhile, thanks to Essem, Dad's license plate number and description were being broadcast far and wide via police radio. Phil Youngdale, the friendly chief of Brandon, South Dakota, picked up the transmission and did a little math: the robbery had taken place in Sioux Falls, the car had Minnesota plates, his town sat between Sioux Falls and the state border. In his Jeep Cherokee, Youngdale drove to I-90 and parked in the turnout just west of the Brandon exit. He examined each passing car. Then he saw it, an unusual cluster of vehicles surrounding a semi. He scrutinized the truck as it rolled by. Peering under its trailer, he noticed a car driving precisely alongside that seemed to match the description he'd heard on the radio. Youngdale pulled onto the interstate and caught up with the car. He radioed in its plates. They were a match. He requested immediate backup.

Youngdale followed my father without switching on his lights or siren. (The Cherokee was festooned with police decals, but no light bar on top.) Dad continued to drive at the speed limit. As they approached the Minnesota border—despite the fact that backup still hadn't arrived—Youngdale decided to pull Dad over. He flipped on the cherries and siren. But Dad didn't stop. Neither did he speed up. He just kept driving. Youngdale saw movement in the car. Dad was rummaging around for something. Youngdale's training told him to hang back.

Finally, just before the two approached Beaver Creek, Minnesota, backup arrived in the form of a Sioux Falls police officer and a Minnehaha County sheriff's deputy. My father veered onto the Beaver Creek exit and accelerated. He cruised through the stop sign at the bottom of the ramp and raced, at speeds approaching 100 miles per hour, down a tiny two-lane road. He passed through town, with the officers in hot pursuit, and toward Luverne. Youngdale called ahead, and by the time they arrived, the Luverne police had blocked the entrance to town with city vehicles. Dad turned off the road into a gravel parking lot. Youngdale attempted to head him off, but Dad made an unexpected maneuver and slipped past. The deputy came up from behind and clipped the front end of the Olds with his station wagon, but he didn't get a big enough piece to stop it. Dad doubled back toward Beaver Creek.

Just before reaching town, my father cut south on Highway 6, in an attempt to disappear among the geometrical maze of country roads. He slammed his foot to the floor, burying the speedometer needle. He maneuvered quick rights, quick lefts, cutting past fields of soybeans and half-grown corn. He turned left at Highway 13, left at 75, right at 1. Thus far, for forty-five minutes and over a distance of almost sixty miles, he'd eluded capture, despite a posse that now included representatives from at least nine jurisdictions: the Sioux Falls and Brandon police departments, the Minnehaha County and Nobles County sheriff's departments, the Minnesota and South Dakota State Patrols, plus officers from Luverne, Worthington, and Rock County.

Finally, in Nobles County, at the intersection of Highways 6 and 15, near Rushmore, Minnesota, a trooper forced my father off the road. His car skidded violently, spun 180 degrees, and stopped, facing the wrong way. He sat entirely in the ditch.

Adrenaline-pumped officers and pleased TV reporters gathered around, taking up advantageous positions. This was big news, after all. Not only did they suspect Dad of other Sioux Falls bank robberies (he would be cleared of all except the last); he was a federal fugitive who for nearly six months had dodged the best manhunting efforts of the Secret Service and the U.S. Marshals Service. He'd even been featured on *Unsolved Mysteries!* Police surrounded his car with their own, using open doors as shields. Dad sat in the front seat of the Olds.

He was trapped, with a decision to make. Since fleeing Minneapolis in January, he'd clocked close to 100,000 miles on his car's odometer, all the while checking over his shoulder for those cherry lights. He'd been utterly alone, bored and paranoid, his twisted thoughts and memories reflecting off one another in a centrifugal nightmare. He'd talked to himself, scribbled notes on the backs of motel receipts. *Sparrow in motel hopping from car to car, then hopping on each bumper calmly and with deliberation, plucking off bugs in the grills. Taking his time on the grilled smorgasbords. Choosing his favorite bugs.*

He'd kept moving, always moving from one place to the next. Motels, movie theaters, coffee shops, convenience stores, those long stretches of highway. The inside of the Olds was filthy. The seats were embedded with soot. The driver's side armrest was black. The steering wheel was corroded with grease and dirt. Shirts, pants, boxers, and socks protruded from the backseat like Kleenex. Dad's car was a compact monument to despair and restlessness. He had been unable to sleep, despite all the unknowing doctors who'd prescribed him Valium and other sedatives to take the edge off. He had bottles from pharmacies across the country—Oklahoma City, Oklahoma; Westminster, Colorado; Albuquerque, New Mexico; and Madeira Beach, Florida.

For six months, he'd been a ghost haunting his own life. He'd crisscrossed the country, visiting places of significance. Madeira Beach sits just ten miles down the coast from Clearwater, where he'd restored the Hinckley sailboat wearing that ratty straw hat. He'd driven to Brainerd and Sauk Centre, where he'd stood before the graves of his family. He'd even checked in on us, his kids. One evening after dinner, my sister Liz looked through her kitchen window and noticed a man wearing glasses looking back. It seemed that he'd been standing there a long time. Then the man was gone. Of course it was Dad, admiring the beauty and sweetness of his daughter while mauling himself with the sad truth that it was over, that he could never again hold her or even say hello.

When Kawaters commented that it was as though my father had "fallen off the face of the earth," he was more correct than he realized. In the backseat of the Olds, Dad kept a paperback copy of the infamous suicide book *Final Exit*. He must have paged through it a hundred times, in front of a multitude of televisions in a stream of crummy motel rooms, searching for clues and camaraderie. Chapter 1. The Most Difficult Decision. Chapter 5. The Cyanide Enigma. Chapter 7. Bizarre Ways to Die. Chapter 11. Storing Drugs. Chapter 12. Who Shall Know? Chapter 19. Self-Deliverance Via the Plastic Bag. Chapter 21. When Is the Time to Die. Chapter 22. The Final Act.

If Dad wished to die, he would need signs, slights, hands shoving him. Such prompts likely appeared everywhere (*If Liz doesn't recognize me, I should die. If the waitress doesn't bring me cream, I should die*). My father was capable of conjuring enormous swirls of sadness. Nostalgia, whether for good times or for all that he'd been denied, was the steam that propelled him. He would page back through the events of his life until he came upon a memory that suited whatever sense of sentimentality he wished to evoke—he stored anguish in a mason jar. And there were so many moments he could have lighted on: Nick, Liz, and me making toy sailboats out of wood at the cabin; Debbie sitting with us on the driveway in her cutoff shorts, her legs splayed out, freckled and covered in paint.

Early days with Mom, the two of them laughing, paintbrushes in their hands, making old walls new. The *Razzmatazz*, that magnificent old boat. Why hadn't he sailed it around the world as he'd planned? Maybe things would have ended differently. Maybe if he'd married Debbie. Why'd she leave him, anyway? Why did everybody always leave?

People sometimes ponder what they'd grab on the way out of a burning house. But what if they were on the way in? What if they were confronted with a short, finite bit of life and had to choose the items they'd carry, knowing they'd never have anything else that mattered? From the Bryantwood, Dad had salvaged two copies of his unpublished novel, *Cash Flow,* and the Code West shoe box I'd mailed him in 1992. These were the crucial artifacts of his life, the gut-wrenching, memory-inducing remnants that would afford him the courage or self-pity necessary in order to do whatever it was he needed to do.

The novel was in the trunk of the Olds. The shoe box was in the backseat, brimming with meticulously preserved artifacts, tools of torture. Dad's collection had been augmented since Seattle. There were the Christmas wish lists from when Nick, Liz, and I were children; the name cards from our hospital cribs; the graded school papers; and the letters. But he'd added things, filled in gaps. Carefully taped to the inside of the lid was an announcement of a writing award I'd won. He'd kept the chilly note I mailed with the shoe box—it had been wadded tight and then smoothed. Now the photographs included shots of Cheryl and Tom and Margaret and Joe. There was the sad, hopeful family photo he'd had the restoration shop create a decade earlier. There were pictures of my father as a sparkle-eyed baby and as a young man. Sometimes he stood apart from everyone else, his arms hanging long out of whatever shirt he was wearing, his chin tilted up, his eyes giving nothing away. There was a black-and-white photo of himself when he was fourteen. He wears a jacket and pressed pants, like he's just come from church. On his face is something like a dare.

The police were surprised that my father robbed the South Dakota bank, given that he was a "master counterfeiter," who admittedly left town with a trunk full of bills. Kawaters would shake his head and tell reporters, "I can't believe he didn't have some type of legitimate money stashed away from his past crimes." But the robbery makes perfect sense. He didn't need the money. He needed the contact. The conclusion. The coda. He needed to be corralled into ending a life that had become untenable.

Dad had been drinking the morning before the robbery. He'd also swallowed a palmful of those pills prescribed to smooth out the rough spots. As the sirens grew louder, he sat in the Olds with the pistol in his hand. He looked out through the dirty windshield at endless green fields on either side of the road. There was no wind, no movement. Time slowed and he drifted a little, detaching himself from the scenario he'd orchestrated. It all felt inevitable, part of a grand scheme that was not his to control. This was happening *to* him.

He opened the driver's side door and slunk out into the grass. He put the gun to his temple and pulled the trigger.

The police weren't sure whether the shot he squeezed off was meant for them. They remained on alert. For more than thirty minutes, they waited out in that 100-degree heat, thick waves coming off the asphalt. An Iowa State Patrol airplane flew overhead searching the grass, hoping to determine whether Dad was crouched somewhere, waiting to pounce with his gun. From the sky, police could see him, lying perfectly still on his stomach next to the Olds. They sent in a trained dog, who approached my father and tore the rear out of his pants. The dog was followed by officers in body armor, wielding pump-action shotguns. They put their knees on Dad's back, attached handcuffs to his pulseless wrists. Finally, they confirmed that he was dead. "The subject is 10–7 permanent," an officer radioed in. "The situation is ended."

When police searched my father's body, they found in his pockets his true Minnesota driver's license and a $5 Powerball lottery ticket, purchased earlier that day in East Grand Forks.

21

It all fell down

T HE MARSHALS HAD repeatedly come to my apartment and phoned. They'd even thought to warn me before the airing of *Unsolved Mysteries*. Yet they didn't call to relay the crucial news that Dad was dead. Apparently they'd moved on to wrap-it-up paperwork, new cases and new daughters. Delivery of the blow was left to the happy, stupid, bludgeoning hands of the media, who banged out up-to-the-minute details and endless *Live Footage!* From the television and radio, news traveled via family connections—from Aunt Mugs in South Dakota, to Mom, to the cordless telephone in my dining room. I don't know how a mother prepares for the task of informing her child that her father is dead. Perhaps Mom imagined me learning it accidentally, from a TV in the corner of a bar somewhere.

When the phone rang on Wednesday evening, I was boiling chocolate pudding on the stove. Stirring the thick, brown, bubbling sauce, I grabbed the receiver and cradled it with my chin.

It was obvious that something was wrong. Mom's voice sounded hesitant, almost apologetic, like she was calling into a cave that might contain a bear. As is her nature, though, she got right to the point.

"Say, Jennifer, I've got some news. Some really bad news."

"What is it?"

"It's about your dad."

I switched the stove off.

"I don't know of any other way to ... Well, he's dead."

"Dead?"

"Yes."

What in the hell were we supposed to say? Mother and daughter, discussing a man who'd ruined lives, whom she'd alternately pitied and despised, whom I'd loved and abandoned. A man who'd given her three children and provided me the very red of my blood. Was I supposed to congratulate her for having divorced him in the nick of time? Would she have been right to say, "There is nothing you could have done to save him"?

We moved immediately to logistics.

"How do you know?"

"Mugs saw it on the news."

"Why? What happened?"

"It's been all over the TV in South Dakota. Helicopter pictures and everything."

Televisions across that flat, range-ridden state had broadcast bank staffers describing the dramatic holdup, officers recounting the chase and the spectacular standoff. They'd revealed Dad's name and criminal history. Mom told me all she knew. The bank he'd robbed was in Sioux Falls. *Federal fugitive!* There'd been a sixty-mile high-speed chase. *On the run from U.S. marshals for nearly six months!* He'd been fatally shot in the head. *Apparent suicide!*

I simply couldn't believe it. "You know, I always thought I'd see him again."

"I guess we all did. I'm so sorry, Jennifer. So sorry."

That's how it began—the endless, unbalanced fall headlong into shock and regret. The summoning of the high, black smoke that blotted out everything except Dad's death. I'd never in my life been as focused as I was on the image of his face at the moment he'd pulled the trigger. I crumbled under the weight of that lonely decision. I imagined the tears in his eyes. One clean shot. Those sad blue eyes filling with blood, turning hard and black. Crouching on the sofa, I pulled a heavy pillow over my lap and stayed that way for a long time. Slow-moving hours drained down a clanging, rusty pipe. I sobbed so extravagantly, I half expected to see Moses with a mop.

The next morning, I woke late, lying the wrong way in bed, fully dressed, teeth unbrushed. I stared into the bathroom mirror, speckled with toothpaste and soap, and splashed handfuls of water onto my face. My eyes looked as melancholy as his. The exact same gray-blue.

There were tasks to be performed. I phoned work and explained to Steve, my boss, one of the few who knew the details about Dad, that I wouldn't be in for the remainder of the week. I plunked down at the dining table with a piece of toast and gazed blankly at the squirrels outside. I wondered whether anyone had made funeral arrangements. I received a call from one of Cheryl's daughters, to whom I hadn't spoken in years, and after a few awkward moments, I learned that a small graveside ceremony had been planned.

I dressed and ventured outside in search of newspapers. I wanted details, all I could lay my hands on. Both the St. Paul *Pioneer Press* and the *Minneapolis Star-Tribune* contained Metro section pieces, which were mildly informative and somewhat contradictory. One labeled Dad's death a suicide, the other wasn't so sure: "A man who police believe was a suspect in one of the largest counterfeit cases in U.S. Secret Service history was dead Wednesday after a car chase in southwestern Minnesota. It was unclear whether the man, believed to be John B. Vogel, 52, of Maple Plain, shot and killed himself or was fatally shot by police . . ."

I learned that either six or ten police agencies had engaged in the forty-five-minute chase, which began on I-90 and ended near Rushmore, Minnesota. One of the articles noted that Dad had been "released on $10,000 bail in February." The other touted his appearance on the "national television show 'America's Most Wanted.'"

The small factual errors irritated me. What grated more was the presumption that these reporters knew anything about my father's character or had the right to discuss his death in the first place; he was more than a sensational curiosity to be vivisected and mused over. Unfortunately, the media were my chief source of information. Kawaters was reluctant to speak after I phoned, crying and hysterical, demanding to know why he hadn't notified me personally. And obviously, I hadn't been there, at the intersection of Nobles County Highways 6 and 15. I hadn't been there for Dad for four years running. There were real clues hidden in his suicide, I was sure of it. He'd left behind a gory, complicated, and very public message. But what did it mean? The interpretation, it seemed, had fallen to me.

The day my sister Liz arrived in Minneapolis for the funeral, with her blond hair tied back and that distraught look on her face, we called the Sioux Falls library and asked a very kind librarian to fax every local story regarding John Bryson Vogel to the Kinko's down the block from my apartment. We'd hoped to avoid calling the town's daily paper, the *Argus Leader,* directly. We felt hunted, embarrassed, and, ultimately, private. In that regard, reporters were our gravest enemy. We retrieved seven pages from Kinko's, certain the clerk behind the counter had read each of them and knew everything. We examined the stories in a nearby park, in the sunshine.

The banner headline read, "Robber kills himself after 60-mile chase." He'd been discovered in the weeds, lying on his pistol, with a hole in each temple. A suicide, without question. As Liz and I scoured the articles in silence, I noted that one of the *Argus Leader* reporters was an ex-classmate of mine from the University of Minnesota. I felt ashamed. Then, as I read, I felt that it was my old buddy who should be ashamed. I noted the cheeky slapstick: "After his parole in 1991, Vogel moved to a western Minneapolis suburb and opened a print shop. But business cards, pamphlets and brochures apparently weren't his specialty." U.S. Attorney David Lillehaug furnished the capper: "Our experience is, he is a very foolish person who flees after being charged in federal court. And now he is a very foolish dead person."

The *Argus Leader* printed an aerial photograph of my father's corpse. It's an atmospheric shot. A cluster of police officers stand in the road near their cars, hoods popped, engines cooling. Dad is lying on his stomach, toward the rear of the Olds. His hands are clasped together behind his back so that he looks to be engaged in an eternal bow. His legs are slightly parted. His head is buried in the weeds or there's a cloth draped over it—it's hard to tell. Dad's driver's-side door sits wide open. The sight of the door bothered me; it represented the beginning of the final act. He'd swung it open. There'd been no need to close it again. He'd slipped out. He'd laid down in the grass. He'd pulled the trigger. The photo was like a diagram. I was indignant that the paper had run this personal and painful image. Yet I couldn't stop looking at it.

Reading the pages in the park was akin to holding a handful of lit firecrackers. I didn't let go and they blew up in my face.

I would become so incensed at the circus following Dad's suicide that I would, for a time, abandon journalism, convinced reporters were nothing more than rubberneckers with all-access passes. I found myself embarrassed at the emphatic investigative pieces I'd written, pretending to expose some baseline truth. No journalist could know the truth about anything, except maybe her own life. More than I was angry at the work of callow outsiders, I was angry at myself. Dad's suicide worked perfectly on me. For weeks, months, I examined the cracks in my bedroom ceiling late into the night, recalling the good times he and I had shared. I blamed myself for not saving him. If I'd resisted cutting him off after that stupid, pointless fight in the car, maybe he'd be alive. I'd tried to help so many people through my writing, yet I hadn't assisted my own desperate father. The failing. A source of almost unbearable pain.

I was on the way to transforming that anguish into something quite dangerous. I toyed with moving to a new city. I all but ceased talking to friends. I sat for entire afternoons on the grass along Lake Calhoun listening to the clanging of the sailboats and envisioning an airy freedom. I wanted to die.

Then, Joe, one of the friends with whom I'd watched the *Unsolved*

Mysteries episode—the brutally honest one—dropped by my apartment with takeout ribs. I could hardly tolerate the mess: every sofa pillow he moved, each track of his shoe, the saucy fingerprints streaked across the kitchen towel. I straightened and tidied and almost screamed. Him—alive, big, fleshy—standing exactly in the middle of my pristine sadness, tossing things about. When I showed him the newspaper articles, when I mumbled that I'd practically killed my own father, he looked stunned.

"Feel bad all you want," he said, "but remember, you're the one left standing here with shit in your hands."

It struck me that he was right. The downheartedness I felt, the megrims, the blind staggers: these were the death package delivered. Memories of pretty cabins and speeches of swans and roses: these were the sweetness wrapped so cleverly about it. I hadn't created this pain. Nor had my father. Nor even had Margaret and Joe. It was an endowment, like the Vogel nose and blue eyes. I heard it, the locust flapping of a thousand ancestors. They waited, floating and bobbing behind me, each peeking over a shoulder toward the front of the line. Grim faces and kind faces. Fancy shoes and dirty fingernails. Each so familiar.

For a long time after, I was haunted by a dream. It was always the same. The phone rang and I answered. It was Dad on the line, except he talked like a salesman.

He started out, "Is this Miss Jennifer Vogel?"

I said, "Dad?"

He answered, "No."

I said, "Dad, I know it's you."

And he kind of laughed and responded, "I have no idea what you're talking about."

I said, "There's something I need to ask you."

He paused.

And then he hung up.

Acknowledgments

I would like to thank Paul Bravmann, Steve Perry, and Julie Caniglia for their unflagging friendship and invaluable advice regarding early drafts of the book; my family—especially my mother and sister—who delved into the past when it was painful to do so; Debbie, for loving Dad to the end; Rachel Sussman and Gillian Blake at Scribner for their guidance and editing expertise; my agent, Chris Calhoun; those police officers and public information officials who recounted and retrieved crucial details; bank teller Angie May for assuring me of Dad's competence as a stick-up man; and, most of all, Rick Levin, my sweetheart and best friend, a gifted writer, who never failed to offer what was needed.